Small City Government

STUDIES IN
POLITICAL
SCIENCE

SMALL
CITY
GOVERNMENT
Seven Cases
in Decision Making

WARNER E. MILLS, JR.
and HARRY R. DAVIS
Beloit College

Random House, New York

Preface

This book is composed of seven case studies in the making of public policy for a small city of the American Midwest. Each case deals with a separate and specific policy problem which came to the point of resolution during the summer and fall of 1959. The main body of each study is a straightforward narrative of the events which occasioned and led to the making of the policy decision, but we have augmented each account by introductory and concluding comments intended to throw light on the problem at hand and to indicate some of the possible meanings of the case in terms of issues and insights into the political process. We have attempted to make each case complete in itself so that little or no cross reference will be necessary. Six of the cases are relatively serious, while the seventh, "The Case of the Bothersome Bees," is by contrast rather light. The Introduction supplies a description of the city and the political structure which form the setting for the cases, as well as several suggestions about studying "decision making" in an American municipality.

No special justification for the "case" approach to the study of political phenomena need be made. This approach was pioneered at least a decade and a half ago, and the various fruits of the case studies presented since are ample testimony to its value. Like most of these, the present volume is offered to serve principally educational purposes. We hope it will prove useful in teaching and learning about American politics and government, especially at the municipal level.

As Harold Stein has written, case studies designed for teaching purposes afford the student an opportunity for vicarious political and governmental experience, to the larger end of developing "intelligent interpretation of governmental decisions and, more generally, of governmental behavior." [1] As compared with abstract general description, the concrete case may more powerfully stir the student's interest and concern, offer more genuine insight into the realities of political behavior, and provide common ground from which to explore conflicting opinions about governmental systems and policies.

On the professional level an increasing accumulation of cases supplies a means for suggesting and testing generalizations about the behavior of people in governmental contexts. The present collection may strengthen the literature by offering a body of cases which, unlike any other series thus far published, demonstrate the policy-making machinery of one particular community at work over a short time span but in a variety of problems and situations. The authenticity of the cases may be supported by the fact that one of the authors was serving at the time of the various decisions as a member of the chief formal policy-making body of the city.

We herewith express cordial appreciation to everyone who has in any way assisted us in preparing this volume. We would like to mention by name the numerous people who responded generously to requests

[1] Harold Stein, ed., *Public Administration and Policy Development: A Case Book* (New York: Harcourt, Brace and Company, 1952), xxii.

for information; but the list would be impossibly long. We also wish to acknowledge the financial assistance extended to us in the latter days of the project by the Ford Foundation through its grant to Beloit College in aid of research in the area of public affairs. It should be clearly understood that the virtues of the present work are the responsibility of many; its faults, our own.

In closing, we would like to pay tribute to the memory of Archie D. Telfer, city manager of Beloit at the time the events related in this book took place, who died while this work was in preparation. Archie Telfer was a sincere and generous person and an outstanding public official.

W. E. M., Jr.
H. R. D.

Contents

Small City Government

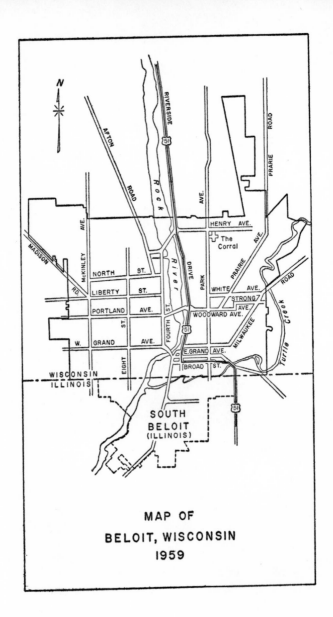

MAP OF

BELOIT, WISCONSIN

1959

1

Introduction

The locale of the following studies is Beloit, Wisconsin—a fairly representative American city of about 33,000 people. It is primarily a manufacturing center, being an extension of the industrial crescent which runs through the agricultural Midwest just below the Great Lakes. But it is also a stronghold of trade and commerce, and it boasts a college and extensive pleasant residential areas.

Beloit is one of the oldest cities in Wisconsin. Foundations of the community were laid in 1836, the year in which the Territory of Wisconsin was created by Act of Congress. At its beginning it was a relatively "planned" community, settled and developed by Dr. Horace White and other members of the New England Emigrating Company. The Emigrating Company was a group of New Hampshire individuals and heads of households who, accepting America's Manifest Destiny, had determined to leave the mountains and valleys of their home state for the prairies of the hinterland. Thus Beloit's character was formed by the solid, conservative values

of the Yankee. This tradition has of course been modi-
fied by the influx during the past century of various
strains of Scandinavians, Germans, Southern Negroes,
and just unhyphenated "Americans."

An agricultural and trading center in the beginning,
Beloit's face was altered with the coming of industry in
the last decades of the nineteenth century. Sharing in
America's technological and economic revolution, the
community experienced the development of many industrial concerns, the dominant ones being producers
of heavy machinery and other capital goods: Fairbanks,
Morse and Company, makers of pumps, magnetos, and
Diesel engines; the Beloit Iron Works, makers of paper-
making machinery; Yates-American Machine Company,
makers of precision machine tools. Only later, in 1921,
was the Freeman Shoe Company established as the
city's principal producer of finished consumer goods.

The impact of industrialization on the character and
social structure of Beloit is quite similar to that made
on scores of other American cities, small or large. Society has stratified principally around the business side
of the community, much as in the "Jonesville" made famous by W. Lloyd Warner.[1] A plethora of organizational life (business, labor, social, religious, professional) has evolved; mobility of population has somewhat loosened the social bonds and the traditional outlook. However, more of Beloit's industry is managed by
locally resident old-family owners than is typical of
other cities.

Certain geographic facts have strongly affected the
development of the city. The Rock River divides it east
and west, giving rise to problems of communication and
integration. More importantly, the Wisconsin-Illinois
border cuts the city off on the south, effecting a legal

[1] *Democracy in Jonesville* (New York: Harper and Broth-
ers, 1949), *passim.*

and psychological barrier to growth in that direction. Nevertheless, there is substantial population and industry south of the state line, in the area separately incorporated as South Beloit, Illinois. Such a situation manifestly complicates and distorts the political, economic, and social life of the community.

Beloit's central business district lies along the river, just north of the state line. Immediately adjacent and still on both sides of the river are the major industries. Then, typically, comes an irregular ring of older residential sections, some of them pocketed in and blighted by the "jumps" of an expanding downtown commercial center. The older residences gradually give way to the newer until we reach the ranch house developments of very recent years, which extend beyond the city limits. The elite residential section lies at the extreme eastern edge of the city, and a large number of prosperous citizens live in Turtle Ridge, east of the city limits and just north of the highway to Milwaukee.

Despite all these changes and problems, Beloit retains many of its older charms and has added some newer attractions. Many of its streets are lined with spacious, turreted Victorian homes and overhung by rows of giant elms. The park system is well developed and maintained; it includes almost a mile of river frontage for picnicking, boating, and fishing. The City operates a well-equipped hospital, a small library, a golf course, and a large modern swimming pool. The public school system has earned a good reputation, and the community's cultural life is enriched by the presence and program of Beloit College, a century-old liberal arts college located close in on a bluff east of the river.

ii

The city, organized under Wisconsin statutes, has a council-manager form of government. The citizens elect at large seven councilmen for two-year terms of office, three being chosen one year and four the next. The elections are held each spring and are nonpartisan— though Beloit is strongly Republican by tradition and only slightly less so by recent voting record. Some years the local elections are spirited, with five, six or more candidates vying for the available seats; other times they are quiet and routine, with only as many candidates as vacancies. Campaigns are personality contests, rarely turning on overt or important issues. Incumbents have a decided advantage over challengers. Usually only 30 to 35 percent of the eligible electorate votes; occasionally as much as half of the electorate will turn out. The prosperous and middle-class wards show consistently greater participation than others.

The City Council is vested with all the policy-making and other legal powers permitted to municipal corporations in Wisconsin. One of the council's principal functions is choosing a city manager, who holds office at its pleasure and is its executive officer. He, in turn, appoints officers to head the various departments of the city government, subject to council confirmation. A Police and Fire Commission with some powers over personnel constitutes the only exception to this clearly defined pattern of official authority and responsibility.

The council's relationship to the Beloit Board of Education is somewhat more complicated. Under Wisconsin statutes the board of education is elected directly by the voters of the Beloit school district, an area slightly larger than the city. It is charged with the establishment, organization, and operation of all types of schools within the district. It erects the buildings, hires the personnel, draws up the budgets, and sets the educational policy of the school system. But when it comes to *financing* all these activities, the school district is merely an adjunct to the city of Beloit. The board may neither tax nor borrow funds but must make annual and special requests to the City Council, which is empowered to establish a tax rate or issue bonds for school purposes. This situation, of course, gives the council considerable influence over school policy and creates the possibility of conflict between the board and the council.

The seat of city government is the Municipal Center, a reconditioned high school building located at the western edge of the business district and betraying its age and earlier function by its high ceilings and wide stairwells and corridors. The manager has been provided with an attractive office, and space has been allotted to city departments, school officials, and other public and quasi-public organizations. But the council has never seen fit to set aside a room for its exclusive use; it meets in the municipal courtroom, which has been more thoroughly redecorated than most other parts of the building.

The council meets approximately weekly: on the first and third Monday evenings of each month in regular council session and on the preceding Thursday evenings as a "Board of Public Works." The board is an official but less formal meeting of the councilmen which transacts certain types of business and holds preliminary discussion of the following Monday's agenda. In whichever capacity it may be meeting, the council sits at a long table placed in front of the judge's bench, a table which provides ample room behind it for five of the councilmen but requires the two most junior members to sit at the ends. To the right, at a smaller L-shaped table facing the council, sit the manager, the city clerk, the city engineer, any other city officials present by request, and two or three newspaper and radio reporters. Behind this group there are theater type seats for perhaps a hundred persons. Occasionally, when an action affecting dogs, trees, or the schools is proposed, the council chamber will be packed to the point of standing room only. But more often the room is only a quarter filled with interested citizens, and sometimes the council conducts its business in the presence of only one or two spectators, or even none.

What do Beloiters expect of their city government, and how do the governors see their own role? Professor Oliver P. Williams has devised a four-class typology[2] which helps provide an answer. In the first type of city the essential and predominant role of the local government is understood to be that of *an instrument of community growth;* in the second type, that of the *provider of life's amenities;* in the third type, the *caretaker* or administering agent of only the traditional duties of local government; and in the fourth type, the *arbiter of conflicting interests.*

Recognizing, with Williams, that no government is likely to fit exclusively into just one of the categories, Beloit's predominant civic spirit probably best qualifies it as the third, or caretaker, type. Some city obligation to foster community growth is expressed principally in zoning laws and in providing a generally attractive climate for business, especially a low property tax rate. The parks, swimming pool, and golf course evidence concern that government should provide some of life's amenities, but Beloit has taken little initiative for these in recent decades. All governments inevitably mediate conflicts in the course of making policies, and the Beloit council does its share, though sticky issues such as the closing hours for taverns and the leashing of dogs have frequently been put to public referendum. But generally the dominant political sentiment in Beloit has encouraged the Council to rest content with providing adequate police and fire protection, building and cleaning

[2] "A Typology for Comparative Local Government," *Midwest Journal of Political Science,* V (May, 1961), 150-165.

the streets, disposing of the sewage, providing money for public education, and operating efficiently whatever other enterprises the city has inherited. As Williams points out, this approach defines the public good pluralistically, in terms of individual rather than collective preferences and allocations of resources, and militates against increasing municipal services and taxes.[3]

iii

The selection of cases for narration and analysis, as well as the selection of those events and details relevant to each case, is no simple matter. Confronted with the dozens of issues and problem situations which face the Beloit City Council in a period of a few months, the case-writer is hard put to choose those few which will be most illuminating. He must resist the flashy situation which is merely full of human interest and drama; he quickly discovers that most of the cases chosen will still contain plenty of that. In seeking to present a true and accurate picture of his chosen subject, the writer should select cases which are "normal" and "representative." The normal situation, says Stein, "is what strikes most people as neither shocking nor highly surprising," and the representative "occurs frequently in a particular society."[4]

Pending the development and application of accurate measures of these qualities, it is asserted as a matter of judgment that the present cases are normal and reasonably representative. None of the actions of the several participants in the cases particularly shocked the sensibilities of the citizenry, nor did the configurations of events seem to cause undue surprise. Most people

[3] *Ibid.*, 156.
[4] Harold Stein, *Public Administration and Policy Development: A Case Book* (New York: Harcourt, Brace and Company, 1952), xxviii.

assumed that the policy-making process "worked" in its usual course. As for representativeness: any case is of course unique in detail, but questions of zoning, street and highway routes, public transportation, protection of public buildings, personal and group conflict, taxing and spending are the ordinary everyday substance of local government. While the cases obviously vary in the frequency of recurrence of the general problem they illustrate, none could be called extraordinary.

iv

The case approach to political phenomena strongly invites a focus on decision making as one valid way of identifying and dealing with a meaningful segment of the political-governmental process. Decision making has in recent years become a recognized and widely used concept in political studies. It may be defined as a process by which the activities of government officials and other interested parties result in the selection of one from a number of available policies or other courses of action.[5]

Analysis of a case in decision making will often be facilitated by recognition of the several steps or stages in the process as identified by Furniss and Snyder: (1) the recognition of the occasion for a decision; (2) the definition and analysis of the situation occasioning a decision; (3) the initiation of a proposal or proposals for action; (4) the review and modification of the initiated proposal or proposals; and (5) the choice among alternative proposals.[6]

A somewhat different formulation suggests that governmental policies and actions issue from the impact of

[5] Edgar Furniss and Richard Snyder, *American Foreign Policy: Formulation, Principles, and Programs* (New York: Rinehart & Company, Inc., 1954), 97.

[6] *Ibid.*, 95-6.

the "four I's"—Institutions, Ideas, Interests, and Individuals.[7] The reader may find these categories convenient "handles" by which to grasp some aspects of the broader context for decision making.

As indicated in the Preface, we have augmented the narrative of each case by comments intended to illuminate some of the significant questions about both the problem at hand and the political-governmental process itself. It may prove helpful if we present at this point several further considerations and suggestions for the reader to keep in mind as he directs his own questions toward the data given. These will bear on the study and analysis of decision making in the particular context of local government in America. Not all of these considerations will be relevant to any one case; and conversely, the reader will doubtless discover still other insights and issues arising out of the cases themselves.

First it should be noted that city governments operate not in isolation but in the context of a national society and a state-and-national polity. Trends, pressures, events far outside the city limits raise problems requiring decisions, or substantially affect the making of decisions. Probably the most persistently significant fact of life in the governmental context is the lowly status of local governments within the American federal system. As creatures of the states, cities and their leaders constantly find their decision-making powers circumscribed by legal and financial limitations.

Despite these limitations, a considerable number of socially indispensable functions and responsibilities have become the province of the municipal level of govern-

[7] Stephen Kemp Bailey, *Congress Makes a Law: The Story Behind the Employment Act of 1946* (New York: Columbia University Press, 1950), *passim*. Also Pendleton Herring, *The Politics of Democracy* (New York: W. W. Norton & Company, Inc., 1940), 26.

ment in the evolution of our federal system. Adapting
further insights from Furniss and Snyder,[8] we may
question the capacity of local governments to carry so
heavy a freight. For half a century, their studies of
municipal structure and administration, political scientists have expressed concern about the capabilities of
local government, but only infrequently has the spot-
light of research turned toward the political, policy-
making side of the governing process. While many diverse factors bear on the question of capability, the
adequacy of the process through which policy decisions
are made is certainly one. Not only is the decision-
making process the focus through which municipal
capacity to achieve objectives is generated and expressed; but perhaps more importantly, the strengths
and weaknesses of a city's policy-formation procedures
are vital ingredients in its total capability. Only through
the study of many concrete instances of policy making
can we build up the evidence necessary for a reliable
judgment.

Examination of the actual operations of a city government affords some opportunity to evaluate the merits
of a particular structure of government. Textbook claims
for the council-manager form—its democratic respon-
siveness, clear lines of responsibility, and so on—can be
tested in a limited way by the Beloit experience. A
related but rather broader question which frequently
crops up in the operation of municipal government is
that of the actual or proper division of responsibility
between administrator and politician, or even among
technical expert, administrator, and politician.

Further, we may note certain insights into the prac-
tical operation of legislative bodies, which may well
apply to the Beloit City Council. As long ago as 1885
Woodrow Wilson, then a political scientist, pointed out

[8] *Op. cit.,* 91.

that decision making may not take place at the point and under the circumstances it is popularly supposed to. Writing of the national legislature, Wilson noted that "Congress in session is Congress on public exhibition, whilst Congress in its committee rooms is Congress at work." [9] Generally, Beloiters expect their council to "make policy" at its formal sessions. Some of them have been mildly shocked at the speed and dispatch with which the council sometimes disposes of important public business. The present cases may raise, and partially answer, questions about the validity of the Wilsonian thesis and the proprieties of formal versus informal deliberation.

It is sometimes observed that public policy may in reality not be made by the official legislature but essentially by other persons or groups. Recently, Charles Adrian has recalled that one of the earliest functions of "legislatures,"—i.e., the medieval assemblies of estates—was not to *make* laws or decisions, but to give legitimacy to decisions already made elsewhere. From his own studies of municipal governments in Michigan and other states, he suggests that many contemporary city councils are again performing this legitimizing function.[10]

Political scientists have long been aware that legislative bodies, far from being collections of equal individuals, are social systems, their members assuming superior and inferior positions vis-à-vis one another. This phenomenon would seem to support an extension of the "iron law of oligarchy," and has been recognized for example in detailed studies of the internal organization

[9] *Congressional Government* (Boston: Houghton Mifflin Company, 1885), 79.

[10] "The Role of the City Council in Community Policy Making," a paper prepared for delivery at the 1959 Annual Meeting of the American Political Science Association, 2, 15.

of the Congress. Furthermore, it is clear that formal and informal leadership patterns do not always coincide. Evidence of this is difficult to perceive, still more difficult to demonstrate and convey; but certain aspects of the Beloit cases may illustrate it for the reader.

Politics and government cannot be understood as simply embedded in the setting of a social system but as woven into the whole complex fabric of human life. For the purpose of analysis, politics (and specifically governmental decision making) must be abstracted from this context; but some distortion is necessarily incurred, as both gross and subtle economic, social, religious, and psychological factors are omitted. This is especially hazardous at the local level, where political life is so intimately blended with economic interest, social status, friendship and neighborhood groupings, occupation, personal prestige, religious affiliation, and so on. In the cases which follow we have attempted to capture and suggest some of these elusive factors, and thus to reduce the inevitable distortion.

Finally, as these studies in local decision making are political studies, they involve more or less prominently conflicts of interest. They will therefore provide, in varying degrees, illustrations and empirical tests of some aspects of standard interest-group theory: economic and other bases of interest, questions of group organization and leadership, reconciliation of competing interests, and so on.

For the thoughtful observer or practitioner of politics, conflict situations requiring public policy decisions raise the question of the public interest or the common good. Certainly much of the public discourse and argument about governmental actions is carried on in this vocabulary. It is widely accepted that the politician ought to make his decisions in the public interest rather than in the special interest of any of the parties involved.

Whether there really is such a thing as the public interest, or whether this is a mere propaganda slogan for what is expedient for the satisfaction of private interests, is a question much debated by political philosophers. Assuming that it is real, how to identify it among the welter of conflicting claims in a particular political dispute is still a challenging enough problem for either student or politician.

2

The Case of the Crowded Corral

Conflicts of interests and values are an essential part of politics, and they often necessitate hard choices on the part of decision makers. At the national level these conflicts may be world-shaking and dramatic; but they occur and must be faced by politicians at all governmental levels. This case study concerns a situation of sharp conflict which swirled around the Beloit City Council. The interests involved could not be expressed in millions of dollars, nor the number of persons counted in the thousands. Nevertheless, the conflict was very real to everyone involved.

It is axiomatic that practicing politicians, enmeshed in a conflict situation, will seek a resolution which is a synthesis of the contending forces. Without going into the question of individual motivation—a realm the political scientist must explore more frequently than he likes—it may be said that politicians are happiest when they have worked out a solution that "leaves them all laughing." (In this regard politicians may be likened to comedians.) Such a solution would incorporate the

16

essential features of the positions of the various contestants in a new, comprehensive conclusion. The quest is for a position to which all can repair without loss of face or impairment of vital interest. Sometimes this is possible, sometimes it is not.

If no true synthesis can be created, practicing politicians will attempt a skillful compromise—"give everybody something." While this might be called a settlement, it is something different from a resolving of the conflict. The politician is acting par excellence as a broker of interests, negotiating the terms of agreement.

Only when it is absolutely unavoidable will the practitioner calculate gains and losses and make a clear choice between the contestants. In our culture he will probably prefer the stronger to the weaker interest; but this cannot be asserted dogmatically. First, the concepts "stronger" and "weaker" involve values, and our pluralistic society is a multiple-value society. Second, miscalculations of strengths and weaknesses do occur. Third, some decision makers will simply prefer the underdog.

While it is hazardous in political science to assert priorities, this ordering is fairly safe: politicians will prefer a resolution of a conflict to a compromise and a compromise to a clear-cut choice among contestants. The course of action a politician follows, however, is hardly a completely free choice. Rather it is in large measure determined by the nature of the situation.

In the northeastern section of Beloit is located Michael Bonafede's restaurant, known as The Corral. Just a few years ago The Corral was a mere tavern. Mike, a handsome young Italian with a flair for business, altered the character of the establishment. He modernized it, hired a good chef, and made it one of the fine eating places—and one of the show pieces—of the city. Since the change, Beloit's business and professional people regularly attend the restaurant for lunch. The "better element" of the city takes "visiting firemen" there when it wishes to show off the home town to good advantage. Mike knows most of his local customers well and addresses them by name when they dine with him, a touch which makes The Corral all the more attractive.

One of Mike's problems as his business expanded has been parking for his patrons. The Corral is located at the corner of two of the busiest streets on the east side: Park and Henry Avenues. Park Avenue is one of the main north-south thoroughfares. It carries traffic to and from Fairbanks, Morse and Company, Beloit's largest industry. Henry Avenue, an east-west artery, connects the northeastern part of the city with the newly built Henry Avenue bridge. Until just a few years ago the area around this intersection was residential, but the opening of the bridge and other factors have slowly changed its character. Some small businesses have located there and, indeed, just across Park Avenue from The Corral is a relatively new multi-pump filling station.

The amount of on-street parking near The Corral has always been limited, but as the area became commercialized, it grew even less adequate to the demand. Only a fraction of the numbers Mike wants to feed each day can find on-street parking within a reasonable distance of his front door. A few years ago, in an attempt to solve this parking shortage, Mike developed two lots for off-street parking. In this project he collaborated with a next-door neighbor (and relative) who owned and operated Bonnie's Bowl-N-Bar, a very popular bowling alley. But this two-lot parking area did not end the problem. Diners at The Corral still had difficulty finding enough parking space, especially in the evenings when the bowling alley was heavily patronized. Though Mike could not prove it, he long suspected that he lost customers who refused to walk a

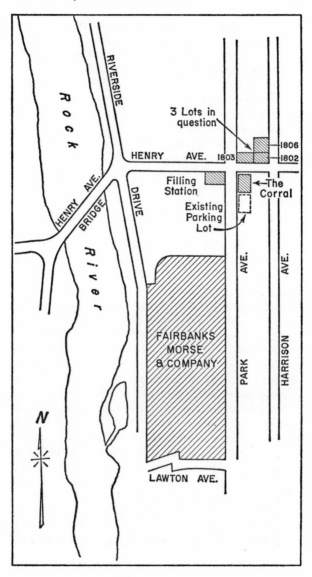

block or more to eat his fine roast beef or Italian spaghetti.

If parking has been worrisome to Bonafede, the traffic which is related to parking has been bothersome to the City of Beloit. On both its west and north sides The Corral is built very close to the street. It partially obscures vision at the corner and thus makes the intersection hazardous for automobile traffic. Though now heavily traveled, Henry Avenue reflects its origin as a residential street in its narrow width. When cars park on both sides of the street, traffic is virtually throttled down to a single-lane trickle. The corner has been the scene of a number of relatively minor accidents, even though the city has long since made the corner a four-way stop.

Late in 1958 the city made a further effort to solve the traffic problem: it forbade parking on one side of Henry and Park Avenues within a block of the Park-Henry corner. This had the intended effect, as accidents were sharply reduced in number. In a special report to the City Council, Traffic Lieutenant Donald Lightfoot noted that in the first half of 1958 there had been six accidents at the intersection; in the same period of 1959 only one accident occurred. But however justified from the point of view of public safety, this restricting of parking made Bonafede's problem more acute.

Even before parking on Park and Henry Avenues was limited, however, Mike had determined on developing further off-street parking. He arrived at this conclusion partly through the urging of members of Beloit's City Council with whom he talked over the problem. The City Council had consistently urged businessmen afflicted with inadequate parking to develop off-street lots. This suggestion was interpreted by the businessmen as a promise that the council would coöperate in making such projects possible. In the fall of 1958 Mike went so far as to propose to the council that he build a parking lot on Harrison Avenue, which parallels Park one block to the east. But the council members were not enthusiastic, for the lots Bonafede wanted for parking were residential properties bounded by residential streets.

The parking restriction on Park and Henry prompted Mike to look once more for land which might be made into parking areas. After some search and negotiation he was able to obtain options to buy two properties lying parallel to and on Henry but fronting on Harrison Avenue. These were residential properties on a residential avenue, but they had these advantages: 1802 Harrison was a corner property, and there were no neighbors adjacent to it who would be inconvenienced; 1806 adjoined 1802 but was separated by a vacant lot from the nearest house to the north. Later Mike obtained an option to buy a third lot directly across Henry to the north of The Corral and fronting on Park Avenue. This was 1803 Park. Together the three properties formed an L-shaped tract.

None of the properties was cheap, certainly not for parking lot purposes. Two contained houses which would have to be leveled or removed. Each was over a hundred feet deep but only fifty feet wide; their aggregate shape made them somewhat less than ideal for parking lots. But with the aid of the city's planner, who apparently considered it his job to aid in such matters, Bonafede devised a way to make use of the narrow lots. With the options in hand and a plan developed, Bonafede had only to get the city's permission to use the properties for parking.

Every piece of land in Beloit is zoned, or classified, according to the use or uses deemed proper for it in the light of overall community planning. The properties Bonafede took an option to purchase were zoned for

residences. Before turning the properties into parking
lots, Bonafede had to persuade the city to change their
classification.

Administration of the zoning ordinances is in the
hands of the City Plan Commission and the City Council. The City Plan Commission is an advisory body to the
council and is composed of the city manager, the city
engineer, one councilman, and four other citizens appointed by the manager and council. The plan commission hears petitions for rezoning in the first instance
and makes recommendations on them, but its actions
are not binding. The City Council receives and acts on
the petitions, and at its discretion may accept or reject
the recommendations of the plan commission. The council's decisions are final, subject only to appeal to the
courts.

To help him present his case to the plan commission
and the council, Mike hired Attorney George Blakely.
Blakely is the well-groomed and personable senior partner in a new firm of young lawyers. He is now devoting
his entire attention to his private law practice, but for
some years he was part-time attorney for Beloit City.
He is well known throughout the city, especially to the
members of the council and to many persons whose
opinions the councilmen respect.

Blakely and Bonafede worked out their strategy.
They agreed that Mike petition the plan commission
and council to change the classification on the properties
from "Residential" to "First Business, Class I." As
First Business, Class I, the properties might be used for
parking. At a future date they might also be used for
other business purposes. Blakely attended to the details
of drafting petitions for presenting the request. One
petition for the change in classification of the two Harrison Avenue properties was submitted in December
1958. A second petition for the change in classification

of the Park Avenue property was submitted in May 1959, as soon as the option agreement for that lot was formally concluded. The plan commission held up action on the first petition at Bonafede's and Blakely's request. In May, when the second petition was filed, the plan commission consolidated the two requests and handled them as one.

The drafting and presenting of the first petition alerted property owners in the area. Those residing to the north and south along Park and Harrison Avenues felt that the construction of the parking lots would render the area more commercial and, hence, less desirable as a place in which to live and raise their children. They imagined all sorts of consequences which might result from the building of the lots: traffic into and out of the lots at all hours would invade their privacy and disturb their rest; the lots might become lovers' lanes or, worse, areas in which boisterous and lascivious behavior might occur.

Property owners in the vicinity felt, moreover, that the building of the parking areas would reduce the value of their lands and homes. Some of them had bought their lots and built their homes when the area was still mainly residential. Others had bought or built when only a few business establishments existed there. All wistfully hoped that somehow the trend toward commercialization in the area was at an end.

In 1959 property owners in Beloit were unusually sensitive to real estate values. The city had experienced a rather sharp business decline in the two preceding years and, though economic conditions were improving gradually, full recovery had not yet come about. In 1957, before the business recession, there had been practically no houses for sale and property values were high. In 1958 and 1959 a great deal of property was on the market, and few sellers were able to get their asking price from buyers. In consequence, property owners were especially alert to events which might threaten to reduce the value of their lands. A number of home owners living in the area, acting under one or all of these impulses, determined to resist Bonafede's move.

The petitions to rezone the three properties came before the plan commission and were acted upon at its meeting of May 6. According to procedure, the plan commission held a hearing and listened to arguments on both sides. The members of the commission viewed Mike's request as a petition for "spot zoning." Spot zoning is antithetical to the whole concept of planning. The members of the commission, their minds focused on the development of a rational plan for the city's development, very naturally took a jaundiced view of petitions which tended to destroy this pattern. Furthermore, the one member of the plan commission who also sits on the City Council, canny, white-haired Herman Schultz, was opposed to the granting of the petitions. Schultz' position on the council gives his voice a good deal of weight in plan commission decisions.

The plan commission made its recommendation to the City Council that the petitions be denied. But it evidenced a certain awareness of and sympathy for Bonafede's parking problem by coupling its recommendation with a suggestion that parking be restored on both Park and Henry Avenues near The Corral, except during the daylight hours of very heavy traffic.

The question came before the City Council for the first time at its meeting of Monday, May 18, when Bonafede's petitions, together with the recommendation of the plan commission, were laid before it. Almost immediately, several persons who resided near The Corral made known their presence and asked to speak in opposition to the rezoning. Kevin Keenan, the short but formidable lawyer who is president of the council, lectured this group on council procedure. He informed them that the council would not and in law could not act upon the petitions until it had held a formal hearing for which due notice had been given to all interested parties. He asked those who wanted to protest the rezoning to hold argument for the official hearing. Then he entertained motions for the advertising of the rezoning petitions and the holding of the hearing. It was duly moved, seconded, and passed that the city clerk be authorized to advertise the petitions, and that the hearing be held on the night of June 1. In view of the recommendation of the City Plan Commission, the council also instructed the city's traffic department to prepare a report on the traffic and accident situation at the Park-Henry corner.

After the official meeting and the departure of those who had attended its proceedings the members of the council stayed on for informal discussion as was their custom, and some perfunctory remarks were exchanged on the Bonafede proposal. Most of the members of the council felt under considerable obligation to give Bonafede much of what he wanted, in light of the fact that businessmen generally, and Mike in particular, had been urged by the council to develop off-street parking. In addition, every member of the council felt that it was to the city's advantage to encourage the growth and expansion of business within its boundaries. Such expansion was a sure sign of progress in civic well-being; moreover, it insured a greater total property valuation and meant in the long run greater revenues for the city. Furthermore, most of the councilmen thought that granting Bonafede's petition was an appropriate way for the council to encourage business. Schultz, of course, was practically committed by the logic of his situation to oppose the granting of the petition. He informed his colleagues that the owner of 1807 Park Avenue, who was opposed to the change, was his personal friend, pointed out that the plan commission had recommended against the rezoning, and said that for these reasons he could not vote with them.

In the two-week interval between council meetings, a certain amount of minor skirmishing took place. A law partner of Blakely called on one of the councilmen, a close friend both socially and politically—the two men also attend the same Beloit church—and induced the councilman to drive with him through the area around The Corral. While the attorney did not formally ask for a commitment, and none was given, the general nature of his visit was clear. At the same time, a letter protesting the zoning change and addressed to the council was circulated for signatures among the residents of the area. Over two dozen home owners put their names on the document.

On Thursday evening, May 28, when the council was sitting as the Board of Public Works, it received the report on traffic conditions at the Park-Henry corner which it had requested from the traffic department. The report indicated that the accident rate had been considerably reduced by the restricting of parking near the intersection. Traffic Lieutenant Lightfoot recommended that the suggestion of the plan commission for restoration of parking on Park and Henry be rejected. He was prepared to compromise with the plan commission on the matter; but the alternative he proposed was patently no solution to Bonafede's parking problem, so it was given no further attention.

On June 1 the council met in its regular session. On its agenda was the hearing on the Bonafede petition. Blakely opened up the subject with a rather long presentation of his client's case. He reminded the councilmen that for some time both they and their predecessors had advised businessmen to develop off-street parking. He gently urged on them the idea that they had before them a businessman who was fighting to extricate himself from his difficulty.

In the ensuing questioning of Blakely by the council, certain weaknesses in his argument were brought out. He did not know, for example, how many cars might be parked on the several lots. He was asked why Bonafede was petitioning for a change of classification from Residential to First Business, Class I, when he could accomplish the same end by asking for a straight "Parking" classification. The council noted that, were the properties to be zoned Parking, they might not be used at a later date for other commercial purposes without further council action; moreover, if they were ever discontinued as parking lots, their classification would automatically revert to Residential. Blakely artfully dodged the question by saying his client had no immediate plans for further commercial use of the lots, "though, of course, that might change at any time." He hinted that his client would settle for the Parking classification, but he stated his preference for the broader category.

Burton C. Peters was chief spokesman for the property owners, most of whom were factory workers, clerical workers, or small shopkeepers. Peters himself was a young business executive with the Wisconsin Power and Light Company. Though at the moment a resident of the affected area, he had been promoted by his company and ordered to Green Bay, Wisconsin, and was preparing to sell his home and move. Peters first called the attention of the council to the fact that over two dozen residents of the area had signed a letter to the council protesting the change. He made sure in his rather slow drawling way that the councilmen understood that these signers were not merely property owners but voters as well.

Peters argued that the granting of the Bonafede request would reduce the value of the properties of those living nearby. He pointed out that many of the property owners had purchased and developed their lands before Bonafede had converted The Corral from a tavern to a restaurant, implying that the rights of the resident property owners were superior to Bonafede's. Peters questioned any necessity on Bonafede's part to develop further parking facilities for his patrons. He argued that the parking lot Bonafede already had was entirely adequate and suggested that all of Bonafede's potential customers could find parking within easy walking distance of The Corral. Although not urging that parking on both sides of Park and Henry be restored, he did deny the danger of the corner, in flat contradiction to the city's traffic department report.

Several other residents of the area also spoke on the subject, but they added little to what Peters had said. In one regard the later speakers damaged their case. Peters had been careful to maintain that all persons who wanted to eat at The Corral could find either on- or off-street parking. The later speakers agreed with Peters that unused parking space near The Corral existed, but they admitted this was so because patrons would not walk from the parking spaces to the entrance of The Corral. Implicitly they admitted Bonafede's need for closer off-street parking.

When all who wished to do so had spoken, Council President Keenan worried the problem a bit. Keenan first discussed the alternatives and sternly admonished the audience that the council intended "to be fair with everybody." Then he moved that Bonafede's request for the zoning change for 1806 Harrison be tabled and, thus, defeated. Before the vote Blakely made a mild protest. The protest was very mild, however, as Blakely understood the signs. They indicated that he and his client were to win most of what they wanted, but not all. On the vote the Keenan motion passed unanimously.

At this point Keenan proposed to Blakely, who was standing nearby, that Bonafede amend his petitions to ask for the Parking classification instead of the First Business, Class I. Blakely bowed to the request and indicated to City Clerk Richard Calland by a nod that he so read the petitions. With this point cleared away, Councilman John Falco moved that the petitions be granted, and the motion was seconded. Then Schultz moved that the request for the zoning change on the property at 1803 Park be tabled. The motion was heard, but an embarrassing pause ensued. No second was forthcoming and the motion died. After some further discussion Keenan called for the vote. The Falco motion was adopted by a vote of 6 to 1, over Schultz's solitary "nay." It was then moved, seconded, and adopted that the subject "lay over under the rules," that official action be postponed until the next regular council meeting two weeks hence.

On June 15 the episode came to an end. When the council met again, Councilman Falco moved that the ordinance embodying the zoning change as adopted the fortnight before be numbered 423, and that it pass finally. No debate occurred; no protests were heard. The issue was put to a vote and passed again over Schultz's "nay."

This small-scale but representative instance of political conflict may raise for consideration several of the many significant issues inherent in the process by which policy decisions are made. What was the nature of the interests in conflict: were they exclusively or only chiefly economic? Did one side or the other have an unfair advantage? Did the politicians achieve a genuine resolution of the conflict, or only a compromise? What role, if any, was played by technicians and administrators in reaching the decision? How close did the resulting policy come to representing the public interest? Different readers will doubtless find in the case various other questions concerning the governing of men by men.

3

The Rerouting of
Highway 51

Classical textbook descriptions of the council-manager form of government emphasize that public policy is determined by the elected council and put into operation by the appointed manager and his deputies. However, such a neat dichotomy of functions is often inapplicable in practice. Councils tend to interfere in the administration of policy, and managers to influence its development. Such tendencies suggest that the line between politics and administration, at least as it appears to those actually involved in governing, is wavering and often blurred—so blurred, indeed, as to constitute a broad zone of ambiguity.

It is true that many problems requiring action can be clearly classified as either technical matters for routine administrative handling or major policy questions for the politicians. But many other problems fall into a kind of no man's land, the degree and nature of their possible political or administrative ramifications being only dimly perceived. Sometimes what was originally interpreted as basically an administrative matter seems to change its very nature and become a heated and complicated political issue. This kind of situation is obviously full of hazards for politician and administrator alike.

Over his twenty-odd years of service as Beloit's city manager, Archie D. Telfer and the ever-changing membership of the city councils with whom he has worked have experienced these ambiguous problems. Telfer, a bespectacled former engineer now in his sixties, has earned the respect and confidence of the city's elders by honest, competent handling of his job as administrator. Generally, his record of sensing and dealing with a politically charged issue has also been good—as is attested by his long tenure of office. The record of city councils in recognizing and dealing with such issues has, of course, been less consistent but on the average rather impressive.

While Telfer believes it is a manager's duty to carry out the will of his council, he knows from long experience that city councils do not always know their own will. This is most likely to occur with a problem whose political dimension is not clear. In such a case councilmen may either ignore the issue in the hope that it will go away, or offer some informal authorization for action to avoid going officially on record. Telfer knows that a nod of the head from a key councilman, or an oblique remark in informal conversation may (or may not!) be as significant a cue to action as a formal resolution. As manager he is then left with the dilemma whether or not to make a decision on the matter himself, and if he does so, what that decision is to be.

Rarely in this long experience have both the Council and Telfer seriously misjudged one of these in-between problems. This case concerns one of those rare instances.

On two successive Saturday afternoons, June 20 and

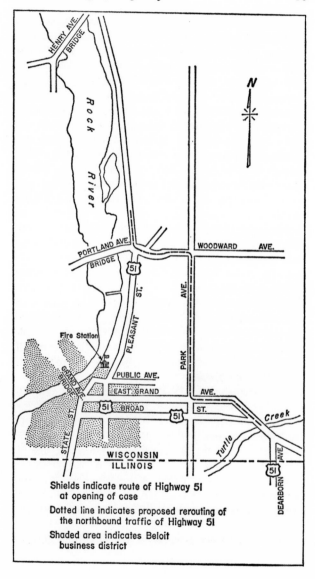

HENRY AVE. BRIDGE

R o c k   R i v e r

N

PORTLAND AVE. BRIDGE

WOODWARD AVE.

51

PLEASANT ST.

PARK AVE.

Fire Station

GRAND AVE. BRIDGE

PUBLIC AVE.

EAST GRAND AVE.

STATE ST.

51 BROAD ST. 51

Creek

Turtle

WISCONSIN
ILLINOIS

DEARBORN AVE.

51

Shields indicate route of Highway 51
at opening of case

Dotted line indicates proposed rerouting of
the northbound traffic of Highway 51

Shaded area indicates Beloit
business district

27, 1959, automobile traffic in downtown Beloit grew increasingly snarled. Local merchants and their employees, accustomed to driving swiftly home, had to inch their way out of the business district. Shoppers who had parked in the city's east-side parking lot were trapped in the lot and unable to move onto the public streets. Vacationing motorists, expecting to breeze through the city, crawled bumper to bumper from one traffic light to the next. Police did their best to untangle the knots of cars and trucks and to restore a smooth flow of traffic. But for several hours Beloit's usually moderately traveled streets resembled Chicago's State Street, St. Louis' Pine, or New York's Thirty-fourth.

The cause of this rather suddenly developed congestion was a heavily increased flow of through traffic over U.S. Highway 51, which is routed directly through the downtown business district. Highway 51 comes across northern Illinois and enters Beloit from the southeast. It moves west over four-lane Broad Street, then turns north onto Pleasant Street, which is one of the city's two major north-south business arteries. Highway 51 continues through the downtown area and out Pleasant which, as it nears and parallels the Rock River, widens into a three-lane roadway.

Since August 1958 Highway 51 had been carrying much more than its normal load, for at that time the Illinois section of Interstate Route 90 had been opened for traffic. I-90 is a multiple-lane divided tollway which eventually will link Chicago with Minneapolis and St. Paul. In 1958 and 1959 its northern terminus lay just a few miles south of Beloit, and traffic from I-90 was dumped onto Route 51. In the summer of 1959 Chicagoans and others were finding this combination of routes the most convenient way to reach Wisconsin Dells and other resort areas of the Badger State.

Beloit traffic officials were not unprepared for the problem. Indeed, the city manager and police department had given it some thought even before the opening of I-90. The congestion, they knew, would be temporary. Wisconsin was planning to construct its southern sections of I-90 in the summer of 1959; when they were completed, through traffic would flow around Beloit rather than over the city streets. But, however temporary the problem period, it promised to be a difficult one. Aside from the inadequate width of the streets for such traffic, police were handicapped with antiquated traffic signal machinery, whose coordination was difficult and unreliable.

The opening of I-90 had given evidence of how critical the traffic problem might be. Prior to the opening, a traffic count on Highway 51 just as the route enters Beloit showed that better than 12,000 cars passed the check point in twenty-four hours; after the opening of the tollway the count jumped to more than 17,000. And, of course, holiday traffic would be much heavier. The possible seriousness of the situation was dramatized a few days after I-90 was opened. A two-car accident on the access road leading from I-90 to Highway 51 tied up traffic for several hours.

This turn of events did not constitute an unmixed disaster, of course. Various merchants along Highway 51 in Beloit were elated with the new traffic. Cash registers jingled more merrily as greater numbers of travelers bought gasoline and oil, hamburgers and French fries, toothpaste, and magazines.

In late summer of 1958 discussion about the problem was extended from the city administration to the City Council. Urban traffic congestion has certain serious ramifications. Traffic snarls may inhibit the movement of emergency vehicles such as fire-fighting equipment and ambulances; and Beloit's central fire station is

located on Pleasant Street at the northern edge of the
business district. Excessive traffic in the downtown
area could also tie up the East Grand Avenue bridge,
one of the city's few Rock River crossings. The city
councilmen seemed particularly concerned with the
image and reputation of downtown Beloit which an
irritating traffic jam would leave in the minds of local
shoppers and the traveling public. Furthermore, serious traffic problems constitute a standing challenge and
rebuke to the professional competencies of the police
department.

The councilmen seemed to be broadly agreed on just
two aspects of the case. First, the city did face a problem and must prepare to cope with it. Second, the flow
of traffic was an administrative matter and already
within the jurisdiction of the city manager. The councilmen were not themselves prepared to decide on a
course of action by formal resolution. Moreover, there
appeared to be little pressure for an immediate decision,
since the full force of increased traffic was practically
over for the 1958 season and would not come again until
the following June. Most councilmen seemed to feel
that Telfer should contact the State Highway Department and "work something out."

Acting on this informal cue, Telfer first consulted
with City Engineer Ed Bennett and Police Traffic
Lieutenant Donald Lightfoot. Then he called in representatives of the Wisconsin Highway Department. At
several meetings in Telfer's office alternative courses of
action were canvassed: all or part of Highway 51 traffic
might be rerouted through the city but away from
the downtown area; efforts to adjust and control the
downtown automatic traffic signals might be made;
extra police might be put on duty on week ends and
during rush hours.

Through these discussions a solution was hammered

out. When the problem became acute, probably in the early summer of 1959, southbound traffic on Highway 51 would continue to follow the old route through the city, but northbound traffic would be diverted to the north and east of the downtown area. Northbound traffic would enter Beloit one block to the north of Broad Street and move westward to Park Avenue, a residential but arterial street. Continuing northward on Park, it would rejoin the old route well outside the business district to the north. The cue for the change in routing would come from the city through Bennett; the highway department would make the order official; then city crews would erect the appropriate markers. It was understood that the rerouting would be temporary and, if put into effect, would continue only through Labor Day, 1959.

When details of the proposed solution were ready in the early autumn of 1958 Telfer presented it to the City Council. His report provoked little discussion and no dissent. The council still made no formal move of any kind. Telfer took one further precaution: he kept the Highway Committee of the local Association of Commerce informed as the discussions proceeded.

The traffic snarl of the following June 27, then, triggered a series of events. Lieutenant Lightfoot informed Engineer Bennett that in his opinion the rerouting of Highway 51 was now necessary, especially in anticipation of a long Fourth of July week end. Bennett in turn called the State Highway Department, which authorized the change in route. On the morning of Thursday, July 2, the signs were erected and the new pattern instituted.

Technically the new traffic pattern worked reasonably well. A number of tourists missed a turn which was not too plainly marked, and blundered briefly into a residential area. Some local motorists were confused by the removal of a stop sign from its accustomed place. But the downtown streets were relieved of the great bulk of the northbound traffic, and the movement of both local and through autos was more prompt and orderly than on the previous week end.

But the relocation of route 51 provoked an immediate reaction from certain businessmen located along the old route. They felt that the change was unnecessary and were incensed that it should have been ordered, particularly when there had been no public notice in advance. The protesters were almost exclusively gas station operators and restaurant owners, and there was one hotel manager. These men saw the intensified traffic on Highway 51 as a thin ribbon of dollars-to-be-spent; if the ribbon moved along in front of their business establishments, a certain percentage of the dollars would inevitably be spent with them. A few of these merchants phoned the city offices to object to the change and tried to contact a councilman or two with whom they were acquainted. The councilman who caught the brunt of their ire was John Falco, a large, likeable, and good-humored man who, as manager of the local movie theaters, was downtown and accessible. One or two resentful voices were heard among the residents of Park Avenue, where traffic had increased substantially.

On the evening of July 2, following the route change which had been effected that morning, the City Council met in its session as the Board of Public Works. Three of the seven councilmen, including the president, were absent on business or vacation, as only routine business was expected.

The question of Highway 51 did not appear on the formal agenda, and no one in the small audience of citizens appeared interested in it. But after the council had dealt with the usual matters of sanitary sewer petitions and beer licenses, Councilman Falco reported

that he had received several vehement protests about
the rerouting and indicated that he himself felt the
city's action was rather sudden and extreme. City Manager Telfer briefly reviewed the history of the problem
and emphasized that the changed routing would hold
for only a few weeks. After some interested but ex-
ploratory remarks from other councilmen, Falco moved
that signs be erected giving northbound motorists a
choice between a "City 51" (the old route) and a "By-
Pass 51" (the new), so that those who wanted to stop
for lunch or gas could come downtown and do so.
Councilman Harry Davis, a college professor newly
elected to his post, suggested that the motion take the
form of a directive to the city manager to discuss this
possibility with the State Highway Commission, since
technically a decision of this sort fell within its province.
But Falco was in no mood for mere discussion. The
motion was duly seconded and passed unanimously.

On Friday morning the "City 51" and "By-Pass 51"
signs went up as directed, and some travelers followed
the old route to make their service stops downtown.
Most of the through traffic continued to move fairly
smoothly over the new route. But the aroused businessmen now had too much momentum to be placated by
such a palliative. They began to organize for action.
They retained Marshall Robson, a respected local lawyer, to prepare and present their case. They began to
circulate a petition of protest and passed the word that
the City Council was scheduled to meet Monday evening.

One of these businessmen was George Denison,
slender and forceful owner of The Spot, a booth-and-
counter café on the old route. Denison not only was
active in the organizing effort, but also took the initiative in the erecting of a private road sign to redirect
by-passing tourists to the business district. In the front

yard of a house he owned on Park Avenue, he set up a large, hastily painted sign featuring an arrow pointing westward to "Business District 2 Blocks: Restaurants, Filling Stations, Rest Rooms." When he installed the sign on the terrace between the sidewalk and the street, the police objected that this created a blind corner for traffic and insisted that he move it back into the yard. This Denison did, at the same time providing it with bright illumination during the night. The police, mindful of the ingredients of valor, did not point out that such a sign in a residential zone was illegal, even though located on private property.

At 7:30 o'clock on Monday evening, July 6, the City Council was called to order by President Keenan, in the presence of some thirty-five interested citizens. The council, now in full attendance, worked its way through a long agenda which included confirmation of two important appointments and action on three large, long-awaited annexations.

The council members were well aware that what the audience was concerned about was an item that did not appear on the agenda. When the formal business was concluded and President Keenan smiled knowingly and inquired whether anyone in the audience had business with the council, Denison was immediately on his feet. He proved to have considerable amateur oratorical talents. Firmly and fluently, but in reasonable tone, he described the economic hardships that the changed routing had brought on the established, tax-paying businesses along old Highway 51. He offered a graphic description of the plight of the motoring public as it tried to decipher the new system, and of the residents of Park Avenue as their rest was disturbed by the noise of transport trucks. He characterized himself as representing "people with a problem," and expressed confidence that the council could work out a solution.

After this display Marshall Robson, the group's lawyer, found he had little argument to add. He called attention to the protest petition signed by forty-five Beloit residents and businessmen and filed with the city clerk, and noted that the new route caused certain minor confusions to local traffic. But otherwise he had to content himself with a reiteration of Denison's case and an official request that the old routing be restored.

The manager of Beloit's best hotel and a spokesman for a large gasoline station also expressed objection to the rerouting. One businessman rose to launch a general and somewhat bitter attack on the council but was quickly quieted by Robson and the others. A resident of Park Avenue objected to Denison's lighted sign and asked what the council proposed to do about it; he said the sign was offensive and moreover illegally displayed. No one from Park Avenue publicly protested the routing of Highway 51 over that street. More important, no one at all spoke up to give support to the rerouting.

When everyone who wanted to speak had done so, Keenan explained that the council and Telfer together shared responsibility for the change, for they felt it would improve traffic flow and diminish congestion in the downtown area. Telfer briefly reiterated some of the history of the problem and reported a week end traffic count which indicated that some two-thirds of the northbound automobiles had been diverted to the new route. Both men noted that the rerouting had always been meant to be temporary.

Councilman Falco hazarded a remark in support of the compromise action of the Board of Public Works and was joined in his sentiment by Councilman Davis. But generally the council was impressed with the audience and its case, especially those councilmen who had not been present for the Board of Public Works discussion. Keenan noted that the summer season was

half over and only a few week ends remained on which
the traffic problem would be serious. He moved that
the old routing of Highway 51 be immediately restored.
The motion was promptly seconded and, without further
discussion, carried unanimously.

After this action Councilman Herman Schultz, who
had previously taken little part in discussions of either
the board or the council, exploded in a brief but angry
speech criticizing the city administration for not having brought the rerouting issue to the council. Keenan
reminded him that the council had been kept well informed of earlier discussions on the matter, but Schultz
insisted that the council should have been asked for
official permission before the highway was relocated.

Denison and Robson thanked the council for its action, and Denison promised that his sign would come
down the following morning. The meeting was adjourned in an atmosphere of general cordiality.

Tuesday morning City Engineer Bennett informed
the Wisconsin Highway Department by phone of the
Council's action, and the department deferred to the
local decision. The Highway 51 signs were put back
in their old locations, and Denison's sign came down.
Traffic began to move again through the old downtown
channel.

The traffic congestion of course recurred, especially
on week ends. Lieutenant Lightfoot did his best to al-
leviate the problem by employing two special policemen
on Saturdays to operate the downtown traffic signals
manually and thus speed the flow of traffic. Telfer,
Lightfoot, and their associates were disappointed at the
council's action; they felt that the decision resulted in a
slower, more nerve-wracking and dangerous traffic pattern than the new route had provided. They were also
considerably irritated by the decision which, taken in a
few minutes, destroyed a solution into which they, as

experts, had poured a considerable amount of time.

The matter is not really a dead issue in the city. The restaurant and filling station operators are again cashing in on the tourist trade. But the editor of the *Beloit Daily News* criticized the decision in his column "Of Many Things," and has run front-page photographs of traffic jams on Highway 51 as it enters the downtown district. Moreover, the managers of downtown banks, department stores, and dry cleaning establishments are beginning to wonder how seriously the traffic congestion is discouraging their customers and otherwise hampering their businesses. When the matter is raised with individual councilmen, the latter reply that July 6 was the time to speak up. They usually add that the whole situation is temporary anyway. Whether this will turn out to be fact or mere political hope, no one can say.

Perhaps no one can say, either, whether the rerouting of Highway 51 was essentially a political or an administrative question, who should have decided it, what were the true interests of the parties affected, and whether or under what conditions the problem might have been better solved than it was. Or, for that matter, whether such an issue ever has a solution.

4

The Van Horn Affair

Many observers have commented on the tendency of Americans both in and out of government to be "legalistic"—to discuss their problems of foreign and domestic policy simply in legal terms without regard to their inherent character as economic, social, moral, or ethical. So pronounced is the tendency, and so unaware are Americans of this habit, that public discussion will commonly proceed on the assumption that a legal resolution of a problem, regardless of its nature, is *ipso facto* a resolution of the problem itself.

Expressions of this national trait are by no means confined to the municipal level of government, yet, perhaps because of the peculiarly dependent situation of the American city, this is where they may be most frequently observed. American municipalities are creatures of the states, and as municipal corporations they owe their existence, their structure, and their relatively narrow powers to the constitutions and statutes of the states in which they exist. Furthermore, American cities are subject to legal suit without their own consent in a way the several states and the United States are not.

Thus, of any proposed municipal policy or activity the first question asked is not "Is it wise?," but "Is it legal?" Decision makers at the local level are probably more sensitive to questions of legal liability than their counterparts at other governmental levels.

The case which follows deals with what is essentially an ethical question. It very quickly evolved into simply a legal question. The legal resolution of the matter laid to rest the ethical question so far as the participants and the citizens of Beloit were concerned.

The problem in the case is the question of conflict of interest—not in the broad sense which defines politics itself, but in the narrower technical sense. It may be stated thus: does a government official have other positions or interests, private or public, which might conflict with the public interest he is presumably seeking and which might corrupt his decisions? A good many statutes and legal opinions deal with this possibility, and we are probably most familiar with it through the quadrennial spectacle of new appointees to the President's cabinet divesting themselves of large holdings in private corporations. But beyond the legal provisions and restrictions a complex ethical problem clearly exists. The present instance is, of course, local rather than federal, and concerns the possible incompatibility of two separate *public* positions.

Beloit's Board of Education is composed of six persons, two elected each year for three-year terms of office. Recently there has been some competition for posts on the board, but during the early 1950's a rather dynamic group called the Citizens' School Committee recruited and nominated candidates for office and frightened off other contestants. The waning of the power and influence of this committee is evidenced by the revival of competition.

In 1959 the president of the board of education was scholarly, mild-mannered Dale L. Thompson, a corporation accountant and administrator. Thompson, a gentleman "of the old school," has a sharp intellect but a soft voice. His leadership was one of reason and persuasion. Other members of the board were Dr. Frank Johnson, a pediatrician; Alan J. Dale, an insurance agent; Leo H. Hansen, an attorney; and Simon Lernor, a businessman. The sixth member of the board, and the central figure in the case, was Mrs. Paul Van Horn.

Ruby Van Horn is a distinguished- yet motherly-looking woman in her late forties. She has long been interested in children and their education. She has children of her own and on their account has been involved in Parent-Teachers Association work. In 1950-1952 she served on the city-wide PTA Council. In 1954 she decided to stand for election to the board of education and she won a seat without opposition. In 1957 she was reëlected without difficulty. Mrs. Van Horn is thoroughly convinced of the value of formal education; indeed, she might be characterized as an outspoken advocate of the interests of the public schools, whether at PTA gatherings, before the public, or before the school board and City Council.

Mrs. Van Horn attended college for two years during the depression. Later she took courses evenings and summers to finish her college degree and completed the requirements for an A.B. at nearby Milton College. When she finished her college work, she looked for a teaching position and found a post in the school system of Clinton, Wisconsin. Clinton lies ten miles to the east of Beloit but still within the confines of Rock County. It is a rather charming, tree-shaded village of 1,138 inhabitants. In signing her employment contract in July 1959, Mrs. Van Horn never dreamed that she might be violating the law or acting in an unethical manner.

Though Beloit is not a large city, it still is of good size. In many of its behavior patterns it resembles the metropolitan center of today more than the country town it was a generation ago. Had Mrs. Van Horn been an ordinary citizen the fact of her employment would have been known to a very few of her closest friends and to only those other persons whom she chose to tell. That Mrs. Van Horn was a member of the school board and an outspoken advocate for the public schools made her doings of consequence to a great many people. Word of Mrs. Van Horn's employment at Clinton found its way to Beloit and then spread rapidly through various social and business circles of the city.

Not only did the news of Mrs. Van Horn's employment spread but also the question which was raised about her employment. The question was whether it was "right" for Mrs. Van Horn to hold a post on the Beloit Board of Education and at the same time teach in a nearby school system. Some of the doubts about the propriety of this eventually came to the attention of Simon Lernor, who had just been appointed to the Board of Education to fill a vacancy. (To fill vacancies on the board, nominations are made by the city manager and confirmed by the City Council.)

Lernor was deeply agitated by what he heard. Some people asserted that it was not right for Mrs. Van Horn to hold the two jobs, and that it was illegal for her to do so as the two jobs were incompatible. Some even said that Mrs. Van Horn's continuance on the Board of Education rendered it improperly constituted and jeopardized its capacity to take legal and binding actions. Finally, it was asserted that were the board to continue to exercise the powers of a board of education, then it collectively and the members individually might be liable in law for actions taken or monies spent.

Lernor was so disturbed by all this that he called his

friend, City Council President Kevin Keenan, and related to Keenan what he had heard. Keenan promised
to investigate the matter and called City Attorney
Gerald Noll. Keenan asked Noll to look into the statutes
and prepare an opinion for him. These were by no
means the only conversations on the matter. It came to
the attention of School Board Attorney George Blakely,
who then had a talk with School Superintendent Charles
Jones and also with Keenan.

Noll went to work and replied to Keenan's request
by letter on July 29. Quoting from an opinion of the
Wisconsin Attorney General, he first established the
principle—a settled rule of common law—that a public
officer could not hold two incompatible offices at the
same time. He further noted that the Wisconsin con-
stitution and statutes prohibited the simultaneous holding of even some compatible offices, though no con-
stitutional provision nor statute governed this precise
situation. Then, continuing in the words of the Wisconsin attorney general, he defined incompatibility of offices as a condition in which:

> . . . there is a conflict in the duties of the offices,
> so that the performance of the duties of the one
> interferes with the performance of the duties of
> the other. . . . They are generally considered in-
> compatible where such duties and functions are
> inherently inconsistent and repugnant so that, be-
> cause of the contrariety and antagonism which
> would result from the attempt of one person to
> discharge faithfully, impartially, and efficiently the
> duties of both offices, considerations of public
> policy render it improper for an incumbent to re-
> tain both.

Noll went on to cite a second opinion of the Wisconsin
attorney general to the effect that the positions of a

high school teacher and an alderman in the same city are incompatible.

Noll reasoned that a possible incompatibility existed in the instant case because the Clinton school district and its board and the Beloit system and its board were to some degree competitors for financial assistance from Rock County. He hypothesized that acts by the Beloit board and the Beloit City Council on matters of a financial nature could and did affect expenditures made by the county, including assistance rendered by the county to the Clinton school system. Decisions made by the Beloit board and City Council, of course, have a direct bearing on the interests and general welfare of the citizens of the city. The inference drawn from these facts was that Mrs. Van Horn might conceivably be swayed by her interests as a teacher in Clinton in arriving at a decision how to vote on school matters in Beloit, and vice versa.

Noll did not flatly say that Mrs. Van Horn had accepted a job which was incompatible with her post on the Board of Education, but he did say it was his "feeling" that a very serious problem existed. He said, moreover, that the "situation could possibly result in a taxpayers' suit" in which the sufficiency of the school board as presently constituted and, therefore, the board's power to reach any valid determination could be called into question. Noll commented that Rock County District Attorney Mark Farnum supported him in these conclusions, but he did not state whether in his judgment the taxpayers' suit which was a "possibility" could be successfully prosecuted or not.

Early in the first week in August Keenan transmitted the Noll opinion to Board of Education President Thompson. Keenan suggested that he did not feel any public debate was necessary, but he pointedly implied that he expected Thompson to settle the matter. At about the same time, on August 3, Lernor talked with Thompson. Lernor, too, wanted the matter cleared up as soon as possible, and he expressed doubt whether he could serve on the board were a cloud of this character to hang over it. Thompson found himself at the center of a dispute of some proportions.

Thompson sought the advice of Superintendent of Schools Jones. Jones, already aware of the question, saw the difficulties in the situation and counseled Thompson to seek further legal aid. He urged Thompson to refer the matter formally to George Blakely and to write to the Assistant State Superintendent of Public Instruction at Madison, Victor E. Kimball. Thompson accepted this advice readily. Pending the return of the opinions, Thompson decided to do nothing.

The Beloit Board of Education met in open meeting on Tuesday night, August 4. Lernor expected the matter of Mrs. Van Horn's eligibility to be raised, but not a word was said on the subject. Lernor was discomfited, and he refused to vote on several motions appropriating monies to pay school bills. Mrs. Van Horn, however, was not aware that her eligibility to sit on the board was in question. Indeed, she did not learn of the controversy until the following Monday, August 10.

On Tuesday, August 11, the board met again in open session. Before the business of the evening was laid before the board, Leo H. Hansen, the Board's most recently elected member, insisted on raising the question of Mrs. Van Horn's eligibility. Evidently Lernor had approached Hansen and asked his opinion on the matter. Hansen had tried to assure Lernor that no incompatibility in the offices existed, but Lernor was not convinced. Lanky, hard-driving Hansen had no wish to give Mrs. Van Horn pain or embarrassment; he merely wanted the board to get on with its business.

Although both Hansen and Thompson desired to

dispose of the matter, they did not see eye to eye on how to achieve their objective. Thompson preferred to keep the matter quiet, at least until he had received replies from Blakely and Kimball. It was conceivable that the question of Mrs. Van Horn's eligibility need not come to public attention at all. Thompson therefore suggested that the question of incompatibility of offices not be considered at the moment but that it be handled privately. This Hansen was unwilling to do.

The discussion proceeded. A couple of times it threatened to degenerate into personality clashes, but whenever this occurred one or another member of the board intervened to ease the tension. Mrs. Van Horn expressed indignation that she had only just been informed of the matter, and she attempted unsuccessfully to trace the rumors regarding her ineligibility to their source. Finally, she spoke somewhat bitterly about people who would impugn her character and yet remain anonymous.

Perhaps the most significant statement of the discussion was Thompson's remark that under Wisconsin statutes the board did not have the power to dismiss one of its members. Only judges of the circuit court of the judicial circuit in which the school district is located have such power. Mrs. Van Horn emphatically informed her colleagues that she did not plan to resign. She said she would consider the matter further only following a legal ruling on it. The board then agreed to ask its attorney, Blakely, to give it an opinion as to its proper course of action. The *Beloit Daily News* published a full account of the altercation.

The following afternoon, under the spur of public attention, Blakely submitted his formal opinion to School Superintendent Jones for transmission to the board. He refused to divulge to the press the contents of the opinion, arguing that any release should come from the board itself, but he hinted that the opinion was favorable to Mrs. Van Horn. Thompson released the Blakely opinion the next day, Thursday, August 13.

Blakely was firm and explicit in his opinion that there was no statute prohibiting Mrs. Van Horn from holding the two posts, and equally firm that at the common law the two positions were not incompatible. In the opening part of his opinion Blakely disposed of the argument that there was an incompatibility of offices by showing that in law a teacher was not a public officer and that, hence, a teaching job was not an office. Accordingly, it followed that Mrs. Van Horn held only one office under the law. Blakely refuted the precedent cited by the city attorney that the job of teacher and the office of alderman in the same city were incompatible. He argued that the incompatibility in the cited case lay not in the fact that one person held two offices but rather in that the individual concerned was personally and pecuniarily interested in a contract, i.e. his employment contract, with the city on whose council he served. Such a situation was specifically forbidden by law.

Although he had argued that a teaching position is not an office, Blakely nevertheless proceeded to deal with the question of the incompatibility of offices. He referred to the Wisconsin Supreme Court decision in *State* v. *Jones*, 130 Wis. 572, in which the Court had held:

> If one office was superior to the other in some of its principal or important duties so that the exercise of such duties might conflict, to the public detriment, with the exercise of other important duties in the subordinate office, then the offices are incompatible.

Said Blakely: "Certainly such a rule does not apply to a school teacher outside the Beloit school district for there is no conflict of duties."

He then quoted at length from the opinion of the city attorney the portions wherein Noll had argued that the posts of Board of Education member and Clinton school district teacher were linked through Rock County. Blakely did not deny this; rather he argued that there was no greater incompatibility between the two jobs than existed between other pairs of two jobs not considered incompatible under Wisconsin statutes. One of the examples which Blakely cited was the set of city councilman and member of a county board of supervisors. (This set of jobs was currently being held without difficulty by Herman Schultz.)

He categorically concluded that "the positions are not incompatible," to which he immediately added, "not improper, not unethical." And he declared that, though a taxpayers' suit might of course be instituted against the board, he was definitely of the opinion that such a suit would not be successful.

This opinion, coupled with a letter from Kimball to the same effect, though without argument of any kind to support the conclusion, settled the matter in the minds of Thompson, of Mrs. Van Horn, and of the other members of the Board of Education. The issue died as quickly as it had formed. No further stories appeared in the newspaper about the incident, though two letters to the editor were printed. After Friday, August 14, no mention of it was made in the daily radio broadcasts.

The same day that he released the Blakely and Kimball opinions, Thompson sent copies of them to Council President Keenan. From the text of the covering letter it is clear that Thompson considered the question settled. Copies of the letter and of the two opinions also went out to every member of the Board of Education.

The episode is finished as far as Beloiters are concerned; the issue is dead. No incompatibility of offices or "conflict of interest" existed. Mrs. Van Horn was vindicated by the Blakely opinion and was "not guilty" of a breach of law—or of ethics—in light of the curious American tendency to jump from one category of judgment to another. It is clear, however, that the ethical question was never properly raised, that it was never thoroughly or fairly discussed, and that, therefore, it was not settled. It cannot be doubted that Americans escape from some very difficult problems by the expedient of resolving them into legal questions and dealing with them as such. Could it be demonstrated that Americans *create* other equally serious problems for themselves by this habit of easy escape?

5

The Beloit Bus Crisis

The American family's practice of using its automobile for practically all of its jaunts and journeys is the root of a host of municipal problems. It is the source of the traffic flow problem—that of facilitating the movement of huge hordes of cars both within and through the city; the parking problem—that of absorbing the hordes within a limited geographic area such as the downtown business district; and of the street safety problem—that of coördinating automotive and pedestrian traffic with the minimum loss of life, limb, and property.

The use of the automobile, itself induced by technological and economic developments, marks a change in living patterns and has created still another perplexity for municipal governments. Up to the end of World War II Americans depended heavily upon public modes of transportation: railway trains, buses, trolleys, interurban lines, and subways. As a consequence of the massive shift toward private transportation, both public and private corporations engaged in the public-transportation enterprise have found it more and more difficult to balance their operating costs against their revenues. Many transit companies across the nation have found themselves carrying passengers at a loss, and many private companies have ultimately been forced into bankruptcy. Such was the fate of the Beloit Bus Company in May 1959. The collapse of the firm precipitated a transportation crisis which, while not so serious as it might have been two decades ago, was nevertheless of grave import for many Beloit citizens. The following case study is the story of how Beloit coped with its crisis.

This case may thus stand as a representative and reminder of the myriad social services whose shapes have been transformed by the technological revolution in such a way as to require governmental concern and, therefore, political decision. Several further issues and insights are involved in the situation. The case poses an important and interesting problem of public policy on mass transportation: government ownership versus subsidized private operation—or is some hybrid solution possible, or shall we do without? The role of values and ideology in decision making (in this instance, the American bias against governmental activity) is clear. Some light is thrown on the internal operations of a city council. But most prominently this case suggests that under certain circumstances much of the policy-making process may take place *outside* the formal machinery of government. Policy making often involves much more than a governmental agency's deciding "yes" or "no" to a formal proposition. Final public policy may be the result of a whole series of interlocking decisions taken by various groups and persons with various motives and acting in private as well as public capacities.

On Tuesday, May 12, 1959, the Beloit Bus Company collapsed ignominiously. The concern had been in serious financial straits for some time, but the extent of the trouble was known to very few persons. On that Tuesday afternoon a crew of workmen employed by the General Tire and Rubber Company of Akron, Ohio, descended on the bus terminal at the southeastern edge of the city. The crew was armed with a court order permitting it to repossess the leased tires on which the buses were running. First they removed the tires from the buses at the terminal; then, as the other buses came in from their afternoon runs, the crew put them on jacks and took their tires. The work was completed the following morning. The crisis came on so swiftly that many Beloiters were caught unawares, and some passengers waited futilely in the chilly early morning hours of Wednesday for buses to take them to work.

Over the next few days the city learned the full scope of the problem. The Beloit Bus Company had leased about seventy-four tires on a mileage basis— a common practice in the bus business. The company had been obligated to monthly payments and had last made a payment the preceding December. The tire company continued to bill the bus concern month by month and, after receiving no response, it finally iniated the repossession action. Only at this juncture did the bus company dispatch two checks, both of them together insufficient to cover arrearages. The tire company returned the checks and proceeded to regain possession of its property. Although at the same time tire company officials indicated that they would accept $2,000 in return for full title to the tires, the bus firm was unable to raise even enough to pay the rental. A certain amount of confusion surrounded the dealings between the two firms, as Lee D. Gale, owner and operator of the bus company, was seriously ill in a Madison, Wisconsin, hospital.

While the situation was unfolding as relentlessly as

in a Thomas Hardy novel, Walter Strong, editor of the city's only newspaper, the *Beloit Daily News,* handed down a dictum which became the cornerstone of local thinking about the bus problem. In the main editorial columns of his paper, Strong stated flatly that, whatever solution might be developed, the city could not, and should not, assume direct operation of the buses: such a move would be bad policy generally and might well necessitate an increase in already high taxes. This injunction was echoed Thursday evening when the City Council, sitting as the Board of Public Works, discussed the emergency situation. The councilmen agreed, at least tentatively and for public consumption, that the city was not in the least interested in going into the bus business.

While the councilmen might well have reached this consensus as a result of their own appraisal, they were encouraged by information supplied them by Ervin P. Jelinek of Milwaukee. Jelinek is the owner and operator of Jelco, Inc., a firm providing transportation for public school children in the Beloit area and in other parts of Wisconsin. He is also a bus dealer, the sales representative in several midwestern states for Oneida buses, and the owner of a bus rebuilding firm at Sparta, Wisconsin. Jelinek appeared before the council by arrangement with City Manager Archie Telfer, having met earlier in the day with a group of businessmen at the Association of Commerce. He was accompanied and introduced by his local attorney, Richard J. Long.

Jelinek's major thesis was that a bus company could hardly operate at a profit in a city like Beloit and still give good service. He argued very persuasively that "people now use public transportation only when they can't get where they're going any other way." As evidence he cited the fact that many other cities similar to Beloit face the same problem. He reminded the

council that in Janesville, Beloit's neighbor fifteen miles
to the north, the bus system had been taken over by the
city in 1953 and had cost the city initially $221,000,
plus an additional $111,000 loss during the five suc-
ceeding years of operation.

Turning next to the local situation, Jelinek reported
that he had reviewed the financial reports of the Beloit
Bus Company to the Wisconsin Public Service Commission in the course of earlier negotiations he had had
with the company. On the surface the records showed
that in the last year the company had lost $10,000, but
the addition of certain operating expenses not fully
reflected in the bookkeeping would set the total losses
much higher. Jelinek's view was that the abnormally
low fares charged—fifteen cents a ride or two tokens
for a quarter—were in part responsible for the company's problems.

At the beginning of his remarks Jelinek declared
rather forcefully that his firm was not interested in
operating Beloit's buses and that he appeared only as
a friend of the city who could supply some technical
information. Somewhat later, however, as he discussed
with councilmen the alternatives which lay before them,
he indicated that he would be happy to investigate the
matter and submit a proposal if the council wished.
But he left no one in doubt that the reëstablishment
of a privately operated bus system would require substantial subsidy from someone. A discussion ensued on
the subject of a city subsidy; the councilmen were able
to restrain their enthusiasm for that idea. Attorney Long
offered the suggestion that in some cities local businesses
and industries help the bus lines by indirect subsidies.
The meeting adjourned with little more than an outline
of the subject explored.

In effect the City Council adopted a wait-and-see
attitude toward the bus problem. It appeared to be wait-

ing to see three things: whether the Beloit Bus Company could get on its feet again; how the general public would react to the absence of a bus service; and whether some local businessmen and industrialists might not take the initiative to work out a private enterprise solution.

In the first few busless days little public pressure for action came from any quarter. Over the week end a petition requesting restoration of service was circulated, and about 180 persons signed it; it was presented to Manager Telfer for transmittal to the council. A few protests were phoned in to the office of the Association of Commerce. Occasionally Editor Strong mentioned the subject in his column "Of Many Things" to ask rhetorically whether the service was worth $25,000 annually in tax money. By and large the people seemed interested and amused but not aroused.

On Tuesday, a week following the interruption of bus service, Lee Gale died at the Madison General Hospital. The same day, the Public Service Commission informed Telfer that the bus company had filed a petition for temporary discontinuance of service. The following day the bus firm filed a petition in bankruptcy in the Federal District Court in Madison, and on Saturday the petition was reviewed and the company adjudged bankrupt. If there were any hopes that the company could get going again, this series of events finished them.

At this juncture the ball was picked up by Eugene J. McNeany, owner of one of Beloit's two large department stores. Mac, as his close friends know him, is an outspoken, sandy-haired Irishman who has for decades directed the growth of McNeany's from the swivel chair of his office in the interior recesses of the store. He had attended the original businessmen's meeting with Jelinek; and, as he thought more about the problem, he concluded that bus service was an essential need of Beloit's shoppers and downtown businessmen and of workers in the industrial plants.

So McNeany phoned Tom Schuler, the short, vivacious native Beloiter who directs the Association of Commerce, and told him that he wanted "to get some of the boys together" to talk over the bus problem. Schuler arranged a meeting with McNeany and together they worked out the details of calling a session of "the boys." The meeting was held June 2 at the Association of Commerce headquarters on Broad Street.

To this meeting were invited Arthur B. Adams, president of the progressive-minded Beloit State Bank; William E. Freeman, president of the Freeman Shoe Corporation; Ervan Chester, an owner of Chester's department store, McNeany's chief competitor; the personnel directors of Beloit's largest manufacturers, Fairbanks, Morse and the Beloit Iron Works; a real estate man; and the manager of the local Penney's outlet, who headed the association's retail division. Others invited because of their specially useful skills or positions were Robert Tilley, a young, popular city councilman; Joseph Kobylka, an alert young newspaperman; and Clyde Bachand, owner-operator of a taxi company. McNeany brought with him his store manager, and Jelinek was represented by his local manager and by Attorney Long.

McNeany dominated the hour and a half long discussion, mainly because it was "his" meeting. He explained his concern with the bus situation and his feeling that it was the responsibility of the business and industrial segments of the community to see to the restoration of service. He warned that were business to forsake this duty, government would ultimately be com-

pelled to take over. McNeany wanted the group to explore ways of resuming service on the basis of private
support.

Most of the audience shared McNeany's attitudes
toward government and its relations with business, but
they disagreed with his analysis of the situation. Only
a few thought the problem was as critical as McNeany
regarded it, and even fewer were prepared to solve the
bus crisis with funds from their own or their companies'
pockets, as McNeany seemed to feel was necessary.

Then Long put forth a more practicable alternative.
Forcefully arguing that the public interest in bus service more than adequately justified a modest city contribution, he boldly advocated a solution which most of
the others found distasteful but might support if necessary: private ownership and operation, coupled with
a governmental subsidy.

There was very little discussion on the desirability
of private rather than city operation. On the necessity
of a subsidy there was little more. Jelinek had driven
home the point that no private operator would be interested without a subsidy. Given an agreement on the
need of a bus service in the city, these two poles fixed
the boundaries within which the discussion proceeded.
Interestingly enough, Long's suggestion, while not receiving much outright support, was criticized less than
McNeany's, which was termed "idealistic" and "un-
workable."

As no immediate resolution of the problem seemed
possible, the motion was made to create a committee to
look into the possibilities and report back to the whole
group—which had by now designated itself as the
Transportation Committee of the Association of Commerce. McNeany was chosen by common consent as
chairman of the study group, and three others were
selected to serve with him.

The study group took its assignment seriously. With Schuler acting as secretary, it began work. The group wrote to a dozen or more large bus concerns, asking each if they would consider operating in Beloit; the results were uniformly negative. It met with Ervin Jelinek and canvassed the situation with him once more; he informed the committee that he was preparing a proposal but was not quite ready to unveil it. The group traveled to Janesville and verified the information reported earlier on its bus operation.

During the early part of the committee's work, McNeany never faltered in his faith that the business community of Beloit would put up the money to make any workable plan function. Others were much less sanguine. Long bluntly told McNeany in a chance meeting on the street that in his opinion a private subscription would never work, at least not for any length of time. As a canvasser for his church and such charities as the United Givers' Fund, Long spoke with a good deal of feeling, but his hard-headed realism failed to shake McNeany's faith. What Long failed to do, however, the Kankakee experience accomplished.

The Kankakee episode began when Schuler and the study committee got word that a private subsidy plan such as they had in mind was in actual operation in Kankakee, Illinois, where a private bus line operated with the help of a limited subsidy from some seventy firms. In order to see the scheme in operation McNeany, Schuler, and two others drove to Kankakee on Thursday, June 18. The four talked with bus officials, collected statistics, asked questions about route and time schedules, and attempted to determine whether the people of the area liked the scheme. On all counts the Kankakee system passed. Upon their return to Beloit the men provided the local press with a glowing ac-

count of the plan, which was published on a Friday
afternoon.

But on Saturday morning the Chicago *Tribune* (Beloit is well within the perimeter of "Tribuneland")
carried the news of the collapse of the Kankakee ex-
periment. Unknown to the bus officials as they were
talking with the Beloiters, the Kankakee community
leaders who were supporting them decided against
anteing up any additional money. The failure of the
Kankakee system not only embarrassed McNeany and
his three colleagues considerably, but disillusioned and
depressed them as well.

The meeting of the Transportation Committee at
the Association of Commerce headquarters on June 24
proved to be the turning point in the crisis. Instead of
the Kankakee plan which McNeany and the study
group had planned to present, Ervin Jelinek turned up
with a concrete proposal, which in turn triggered a
spirited discussion of alternatives, and the meeting ultimately took on a really optimistic tone.

Jelinek proposed that his firm establish a bus service
for the city; that the buses run every half hour during
rush periods and hourly at slack times; that the fares
of necessity be raised; and that the company provide
new or improved buses to the community. In its details
the plan coincided with McNeany's thinking and with
that of most of the others present. But Jelinek had
miscalculated the temper of the group on the subject of
finances, for he suggested, in effect, that he would furnish the service if the Transportation Committee assumed the financial risks of the enterprise with the possibility of sharing any profits. This aspect the committee rejected out of hand.

The discussion, however, provoked a series of other
ideas. It became clear that Jelinek was asking for an
annual subsidy on the order of $5,000 to $8,000,

whereas heretofore all thought and discussion of a subsidy had revolved around the $20,000 to $30,000 Janesville figures. The substantially lower figure seemed to
open up new possibilities. Bachand, the taxi company
owner, "thought out loud" about a jitney service by the
cab companies which might operate at a twenty-five-
cent fare and a modest subsidy. His suggestion caught
interest, and he was asked to explore it further and report back.

Then Jelinek, his first proposal rejected, suggested the
possibility of the city's obtaining the bus franchise,
buying the buses, and then selling them back to a private operator over a ten-year period. This scheme promised private ownership and operation of the system with
a reasonable and indirect subsidy from the city. The
general feeling was that this scheme also should be pursued. Long was asked to put both Jelinek proposals in
writing for later consideration by the committee.

Seven days later Long submitted in writing not these
two but a third proposition to the committee. Jelinek, on
third thought, offered to furnish the proposed service
and assume all the risk himself if someone would supply him with the following: an inside, heated storage
area to accommodate six buses, and a repair area for
four; the privilege to install underground gasoline tanks
on the same property; room for a modest office and
drivers' waiting area; and outdoor parking space for
twenty-five buses (which would partly subsidize Jelco's
school bus operation also). Jelinek asked that any agreement on this proposition be written for a one-year trial
period. He consented to maintain routes similar to the
old ones, but he put the committee on notice that he
intended to give service to areas surrounding Beloit as
well as the city proper. He proposed to begin operations
September 1, if the offer proved satisfactory.

In drafting the letter, Long was deliberately vague as

to where the facilities, or their cash equivalent, were to come from. Jelinek himself was opposed to the principle of governmental subsidies and would have preferred to deal with other businessmen; but Long, in closer touch with local realities, knew that a city subsidy was a more distinct possibility than a private one.

On receipt of this July 1 letter, Schuler contacted McNeany and McNeany in turn called Freeman. Together they went over the Jelinek proposal in detail and agreed that it was the most feasible scheme in prospect. They saw nothing to be gained by reconvening the Transportation Committee. So they determined to push ahead for a deal with Jelinek, despite the fact that they had heard nothing from Bachand about the alternative jitney service. Jelinek impressed them as a tough-minded, responsible businessman, whose operation could be depended upon; he offered a familiar kind of service; and they were growing tired of false starts toward relieving the crisis.

Next McNeany, Freeman, and Schuler went to work to determine which particular facilities should be furnished to Jelinek and how they should be paid for. McNeany contacted Lee Gale's father, A. P. Gale, who owned the building which had housed the ill-fated Beloit Bus Company. McNeany convinced him, though he wanted to sell the property, that he should rent it instead for $500 a month. McNeany could not immediately offer Gale a tenant, but he could hint strongly that Jelinek under the auspices of the Transportation Committee or the City, would be mightily interested. McNeany took Long to see the building and secured from him assurance that the building generally met Jelinek's requirements.

The second question—who would foot the bill—was easily answered; gradually everyone had come to recognize that there was no possibility of a private subscription, and the alternative was a municipal subsidy. It was agreed to press the city fathers to lease the bus terminal from Gale and make it available to Jelinek.

These questions settled, McNeany and Freeman paid a call on Council President Kevin Keenan. Keenan seemed favorably disposed to the proposal. But as a lawyer and a councilman conscious of a city government's limitations he raised the question of the legal authority of the City to enter such an agreement. City Attorney Gerald Noll was asked for an opinion on the point. After a quick look at the statutes, Noll rendered a "horseback" judgment that the scheme could not be legally entered into by the City, though he did not consider this hasty opinion as definitive. When this reading of the law was relayed to Long, Long exploded in his soft but determined tone, "Hell, yes, it can be done." He argued that the deal was fair and above board and demonstrably in the public interest.

On the night of July 30 McNeany, Freeman, and Schuler went before the Board of Public Works to hand it the Jelinek plan. Actually the board had finished its business and had formally adjourned when the three businessmen appeared by prearrangement to talk "off the record" with the board (or council) members. They presented Long's letter which spelled out the Jelinek proposal in detail and suggested that the City supply the facilities Jelinek required. They pointed out that Gale was prepared to lease his building and that Long had approved it. They noted the suggested rental of $6,000 per year and that to fulfill Jelinek's conditions the City would have to lay out only about another $1,000 for heating the building. Thus, for $7,000, Beloit would get a bus service comparable to Janesville's, but at just a fraction of the cost. In general the councilmen reacted favorably; the plan seemed a reasonable way out of the city's difficulty and $7,000 a reasonable price to pay for maintaining a traditional city service.

The Noll opinion on the legality of the proposition was known to the councilmen and gave rise to some discussion. There was general recognition that a question did exist, but also optimism that "a way out could be found." In the interim Noll had done some research on the matter and he contributed the information that another Wisconsin city had entered into a somewhat similar agreement with a private concern. He was directed to contact the officers of the Wisconsin Public Service Commission and the Wisconsin League of Municipalities to ask their opinions on the legality of the Jelinek arrangement.

The councilmen now raised questions that were more "political" in nature. For instance, asked Herman Schultz, what fare would Jelinek charge? McNeany and Freeman thought the initial rates would be a straight twenty cents a ride, even though this would result in a deficit; the bus users would have to be wooed back to riding again and educated to a higher fare.

The question of routes to be followed was also raised. Councilmen were especially concerned over the suggestion that the new company would serve suburban areas outside the city limits. Were city taxpayers being asked to subsidize these outsiders who already were not paying their fair share of the costs of municipal services? McNeany and Freeman could only answer that Jelinek intended to find his customers wherever he could, that this seemed to them a businesslike approach which might possibly mean the difference between a subsidy and no subsidy in future years. The councilmen agreed, however, that in the formal open negotiations nothing would be said about routes. The councilmen further agreed that Jelinek would furnish the city with financial statements at no less than three-month intervals so that the status of the operation could be followed.

The council could not, of course, take formal action at this point. But the members clearly indicated their desire that City Manager Telfer proceed to develop the plan in full and lay the proper resolutions before them as soon as possible.

The legal snarl was quickly and satisfactorily cleared. The Public Service Commission reported that it had accepted similar municipal-utility company agreements in the past. The legal counsel for the League of Municipalities wrote an extended opinion in which he argued for the validity of the arrangement. Noll passed this information on to Telfer and the council, adroitly suggesting that since the contracts would run for only a year, it seemed unlikely that any possible challenge to them could be fully prosecuted through the courts before their expiration!

The work of drafting the agreements was pushed. Gale's attorney drafted the lease agreement between Gale and the City while Long, in consultation with Noll, drew up the agreement between the City and Jelinek.

At this stage McNeany and Freeman retired from the field. Schuler was active only to the extent of passing on word of developments to various members of the Transportation Committee as he chanced upon them on the streets or in the lobbies of the Hilton Hotel or the State Bank. When the news reached Clyde Bachand, he was left rather disappointed and unhappy; he had gone to considerable trouble and expense to investigate various jitney services, but he was now not to have his plan considered.

When the Board of Public Works met on September 3, an item relating to the agreements with Jelinek was on its agenda. The board members scanned the lease and other agreements which had been laid before them.

Only five of the seven members were present. During the rather desultory discussion of the matter, Gordon Merchant, a Fairbanks, Morse employee and the most cost-conscious of the councilmen, noted that the agreement called not for a City contribution of $1,000 for heating the bus terminal but for City assumption of the burden of heating the building regardless of cost. Some other members joined him in questioning this open-ended clause. But it was agreed that the actual cost would probably not be much different, and that City officials would keep close check on that expense.

Councilman Herman Schultz raised the further objection that the building rental was too high and that some negotiations were in order. He felt that the whole matter was being handled too quietly and that the council should hold a public hearing to determine what the people thought. Keenan exploded at this suggestion. "Let's get it on the streets," he snapped, referring to the bus service. He felt too much time had been lost already and that no more delay was warranted under any pretext.

While he had the floor, Keenan used the opportunity to deliver a lecture to the five or six citizens in the council chamber and to the citizenry of Beloit through the news media. He wanted it clearly understood, he said, that the City of Beloit was not entering the bus business and that the city government would have nothing to do with the operation of the buses, their rates, hours, or routes. Councilmen wanted no phone calls from irate citizens as to why the buses were late or didn't stop at a particular corner. He emphasized the necessity that the people make full use of the bus system. "If the people of Beloit don't support such a plan as the present one," he warned somewhat ominously, "it would be very difficult a year from now for the council to negotiate another contract." His message off his chest, Keenan

asked rather suddenly if there were any further discussion. Hearing none, he informed his colleagues that the
matter would be up for official action at the next regular council meeting.

The council met on the following night, having
moved up it's regular session to avoid meeting on Labor
Day. The necessary resolutions to authorize the execu-
tion of the agreements and the payment of funds for the
rent and heating of the bus terminal had been prepared. They were laid before the council, moved, seconded, and adopted without dissent—and without further discussion.

On learning of the council's action, Jelinek expressed
his pleasure at the decision. He stated for the press that
if his firm broke even during the one-year period he
would be happy, though presumably as a businessman
he had rosier hopes for the long haul. After the execu-
tion of the several agreements he quickly proceeded
with the necessary moves toward getting the buses on
the streets. He incorporated as Beloit City Bus Lines
and arranged with the Public Service Commission for a
temporary permit to serve Beloit. He bought nine buses
in various states of repair from the old Beloit Bus Company and sent seven of them to his Sparta shop to be
refurbished. He planned routes, set a fare of twenty
cents, and publicized the "grand re-opening." Jelinek
hoped to begin operations by October 12, but it was
not until October 19 that the first buses went out on
their new rounds, ending the transportation crisis which
cost Beloit 160 days without public conveyances.

Thus the city of Beloit experienced in microcosm a
serious problem thrust upon the nation by technological
and social change and arrived at a public policy which
provided a temporary solution. The solution itself
moved the community, reluctantly and against its preference, one small step away from private and toward

governmental responsibility for the operation of an important public service activity.

As for the political process—the *way* in which the policy was arrived at—private citizens and groups participated in a most prominent and vigorous manner. In the long series of actions and decisions which resulted in the City Council's formal agreements with Jelinek, the role of the public officials seems to have been minimal. Private persons and interest groups appear to have dominated in varying degree the various stages by which the policy decision was reached. Whether or not such a procedure is typical is a question which may be answered as sufficient studies of decision making accumulate. Whether, or under what circumstances, it is right and proper for government policy makers to defer to the initiative of private persons or groups is a question which may not be answered definitively.

6

The Emergency Fire
Protection Appropriation

The substance of this case is the process by which the civic leaders of Beloit decided at a time of sharpened public concern whether, how, and how much to increase the protection of the city's public school buildings against fire. The case suggests several insights and questions of more general interest to the student of municipal decision making, of which two may be raised explicitly.

First, the case illustrates the impact of events, interests, and persons well beyond the boundaries of the city on municipal policy making. It is, of course, elementary that American cities are constitutionally dependent upon their respective states for their powers, their finances, and their very existence. It is not always so clearly recognized that in a rapidly shrinking and interdependent world the political processes of city government, no less than of state and national governments, are influenced by external forces. While for certain analytical purposes it may be justifiable to isolate a

73

smaller political community and study its internal power
structure, it should be borne in mind constantly that
trends and events of the larger environment often affect
the city crucially. In the present case the issue was
raised by an event which occurred a hundred miles
away from Beloit, and interests from outside the city
played important roles in solving it.

Second, the case raises interesting questions about the
location and acceptance of responsibility for public
decisions, especially in a council-manager system. It is
well established that municipal governments are responsible for providing reasonable protection to citizens and
their property, including protection against fire hazards.
This obligation applies with special strength to public
properties such as municipal buildings. When there is
added, as in the case of school buildings, the element of
human lives, indeed the lives of children, then the function is potentially charged with tremendous public sensi-
tiveness and emotion.

Absolute security against any given hazard is impossible in this world, and it is a simple fact that one hundred percent safety for school children's lives cannot be
purchased at any price. Experts may be able to inform
policy makers on what is technically possible or ideally
desirable to maximize safety. But then, practically
speaking, the deciding officials must measure whatever
they judge to be a reasonable program of protection
against at least two further limiting factors: the citizens'
ability and their willingness to pay. In a context of so
many imponderable fears, risks, and values officials may
understandably shrink from the moral and political responsibility of choosing and deciding.

Who, in the following situation, holds the specific
responsibility for decision on this kind of fearsomely
ticklish question? The elected members of the school
board, charged with building and maintaining schools

and, therefore, with fire protection installations? The fire department, expected to advise and coöperate in prevention programs as well as to act in case these programs fail? The City Council, responsible for the school budget and, therefore, for financing or vetoing protection projects? Theoretically, in a council-manager system, responsibility is always and completely focused. The student might ask himself if, practically, this centering and focusing of responsibility always obtains.

On December 1, 1958, a fire broke out in a stairwell in one wing of Our Lady of the Angels School in Chicago, Illinois. Heavy smoke and fire gases spread up the stairwell and through a second-floor corridor of this Roman Catholic elementary school. Minutes later, with a muffled roar, the fire gases exploded and the corridor burst into flames. The smoke, heat, and then the fire itself cut off the normal escape route for several hundred children and their instructors. Ninety children and three nuns lost their lives. Seventy-seven children were seriously injured.

News of the fire and the loss of life was carried across the nation by press, radio, and television, horrifying millions of Americans. Many citizens wanted to know how the fire had happened and whether such a disaster were possible in the schools of their own cities. Beloit citizens, like their fellows elsewhere, wanted to know not only the "how" of the fire but especially "can it happen here?"

Certain Beloit officials and well-informed citizens were, of course, already aware of the general scope and character of the school fire protection problem. The Beloit Board of Education maintains and operates thirteen elementary schools, two junior high schools, and one senior high school. The senior high school is located in a modern structure just ten years old, and there are

few fire hazards there. The two junior high schools and
all but a few of the elementary schools, however, are
located in old buildings ranging from twenty-five to
eighty-eight years in age. The old buildings are less fire
resistive than the senior high school, and, generally
speaking, the danger is directly proportionate to the age
of the buildings. Thus, Beloit officials and others were
aware of a fire protection problem even before the Chicago tragedy.

The Chicago tragedy, however, did provoke two different groups to take a new look at the Beloit problem.
The first of these was the City Fire Department, and
especially its chief, Glen Davis, and its chief fire inspector, Anton Scodwell. The second group was a citizen
action group styled the School Building Advisory Committee. The tragedy also provoked a private citizen,
Stuart D. Klinger, to call for action to make the schools
safer.

The City Fire Department had an established practice of inspecting the public school buildings twice each
year. In light of the intense public interest in the question of fire protection, Davis and Scodwell decided to
make a new inspection late in December 1958, although
a regular inspection had been completed just the preceding October. While a certain sense of urgency acti-
vated the two men, the inspections were carried out in
the knowledge that even the older buildings had been
modernized to an extent and met the minimum fire
safety requirements of the Wisconsin State Industrial
Commission.

On January 26, 1959, Davis and Scodwell prepared
a set of recommendations for further reducing the fire
hazards in the schools and transmitted them to Burton
Williams, business manager of the public schools. The
two men explicitly called attention to the fact that they
had found "compliance with minimum fire safety stand-

ards of the state fire code in all cases." The two men felt, however, that additional safety devices or procedures were desirable for the seven oldest elementary school buildings.

Specifically, Davis and Scodwell recommended the installation of one hundred percent automatic sprinkler systems in these seven schools, the enclosing of all open stairways with doors giving at least one hour protection, the installation of fire escapes where necessary, and the fixing of window screens on all classroom windows so that they might be removed easily from the inside. They also proposed the establishment of a monitoring system in each school. By this latter proposal the two men meant the stationing of older children at desks in the halls of the several schools as fire lookouts. The children were to serve on a rotating basis, but it was the chief's thought that some child or children would be on duty at all times. The letter was written in a spirit of realism: obliquely referring to the depressed condition of Beloit's economy, the two men concluded with the sentence, "We are giving these recommendations to you, so that they might be considered at such a time when economic conditions in the city have improved."

The School Building Advisory Committee (S.B.A.C.) started off on much the same tack as the fire department officials. The S.B.A.C. was a group which had been formed in the early 1950's for the purpose of investigating and making recommendations on the building needs of the public school system, and was composed of school board representatives and leading citizens. The committee's focus was on long-range planning for general space requirements, but consideration had been given in the immediate past to the replacement of the old elementary school buildings and the development of plans for a new junior high school.

The S.B.A.C. decided in January 1959 to inspect

again all the older elementary schools for fire safety conditions. Three subcommittees were created, and each was made responsible for inspection of a particular school; other subcommittees and inspections were contemplated to the date that a new special city-wide committee was created which took up this work. The temper of the subcommittees, and of the parent S.B.A.C., may be judged by comments made in or appended to the reports which were written. In regard to one of the very oldest of the elementary schools the comment was made by a member of the inspecting subcommittee that:

> The Beloit School Board would, in my opinion, be making a mistake if it put monies the like of, say, $10,000 or more into trying to make a silk purse out of this sow's ear, if there is any possibility of replacing the building in the next four or five years.

The S.B.A.C. subcommittee report on the Hackett elementary school is typical of the three reports, and its picture of Hackett can well stand as representative of the seven older schools. The Hackett school consists of two buildings: an original two-storied structure built in 1895 and a single-story addition erected in 1958. The original building contains eight classrooms, four on each floor, and so far as fire hazards exist at this school, they exist in connection with this old structure.

The 1895 building is wood with a brick veneer. Its interior walls and floors are of wood construction. Both floors are supported by wood beams, except for that portion above the boiler room in the full basement. On each floor of the building the four classrooms open onto a large central hall. The two floors are connected by wide, open wooden stairways. Throughout the classrooms and stairways there is a wooden wainscoting extending approximately two feet from the floor. The fire hazard is due primarily to the fact that the wood in the building is tinder dry.

It should be noted that certain steps had already been taken to minimize the fire hazard. Two second-story classrooms were equipped with outside exits to fire escapes; boiler room improvements were made; old electrical wiring was replaced; and an incinerator, built for the disposal of wastepaper, was housed in a separate structure at a safe distance from the original building. Besides these structural changes and improvements, school authorities and city officials had taken precautions to minimize the risks involved. The children were well trained in building evacuation procedures. Janitorial help kept the building spotlessly clean and free from accumulations of waste and other inflammable material. City Fire Department personnel, through their regular inspections, had become familiar with the building's layout and room arrangement. On balance, the Hackett school was a "fair fire risk."

Stuart Klinger has lived in Beloit most of his life. He was educated in the Beloit public schools and at Beloit College. Although he is an engineer by profession, he has long been interested in fire protection and firefighting. So avid is his interest that he has prepared and published technical articles on fire-fighting in professional journals devoted to the subject. About a dozen years ago he served a single term on the Beloit City Council and as a councilman fought hard for the interests of the fire department.

On January 18, 1959, after waiting in vain for evidence of discussion of Beloit's public school fire problem (no story appeared about either fire department or S.B.A.C. activities during December and January in the city's one newspaper, the *Beloit Daily News*), Klinger wrote a lengthy letter to Dale Thompson, president of the Board of Education. Deploring what he thought to be a lack of interest in the city about its school building fire problem, he attempted to arouse such interest. He noted that certain elementary schools contained a veritable "forest of wood," that stairwells were unenclosed, and that no sprinkler systems had been installed.

Klinger pointedly remarked that fire officials in Rockford, Illinois, sixteen miles south of Beloit, had made recommendations for reducing the fire hazards in the city schools and that Rockford school authorities had already let contracts on the basis of the recommendations. In closing, Klinger offered his services to Thompson and the school board. Thompson was impressed with the letter and had it duplicated and circulated widely.

Other citizens were concerned about the school fire problem, and about a dozen persons turned out for the February 10 meeting of the Board of Education. Because of the interest shown, the chief topic of discussion was the fire protection problem. The dominant notes of the meeting were anxiety and urgency. There was little criticism of the fire department or the school authorities, but all seemed to feel that the situation was critical enough to warrant the establishment of a new study-and-action committee. On the basis of the discussion, school board member Dr. Lester B. McAllister, Jr. moved that the board authorize Superintendent of Schools Charles Jones, who was absent from the meeting, to create an Emergency Committee for Fire Protection in the Schools. He coupled with this a proposal to investigate a monitoring system which had been suggested by the fire department. The motion was unanimously adopted by the board.

Jones set to work almost immediately to select the membership of the emergency committee. In late February and early March letters of invitation went out to approximately thirty persons, and twenty-six responded favorably. The roster of the committee included Arthur B. Adams, president of the Beloit State Bank; Ervan Chester, department store owner; Ernest Smith, general manager of a second department store, McNeany's; Walter Strong, editor of the city's newspaper; Dr. Herbert Raube; the Reverend Dale Strong; E. R. McGinnis, manager of the local office of the Wisconsin Telephone Company; and some civic-minded mothers and housewives, Mrs. William Miller, Mrs. William Sorenson, and Mrs. Miller Upton. Also included in the group was Stuart Klinger. The S.B.A.C. continued its school inspections, but when the new group began to work, the S.B.A.C. retired from the field. The monitoring system idea was quietly shelved when Jones privately explained the difficulties from an academic point of view which inhered in it.

The emergency committee, as broadly based as it was, failed to reflect one important interest. No person representing the city administration generally, nor the fire department specifically, was invited. This was an oversight which gave rise to some hard feelings at the fire house and Municipal Center. The oversight was doubly unfortunate because of the existence at the time of antagonism between the City Council and the school board. The two bodies had clashed rather sharply the preceding December over the school budget, the preparation of which is the responsibility of the school board but the adoption of which is the prerogative of the council. In choosing the membership of the emergency committee, an attempt was made to take the subject "out of politics," but in the political climate of early 1959 this smacked of an attempt to outflank the City Council.

The first meeting of the emergency committee was held at the Municipal Center on March 18. School

Superintendent Jones opened the meeting by reading
the resolution authorizing him to create the committee.
The chairman of the S.B.A.C. was on hand, and he outlined the work of his organization. He argued the need
for this new special emergency committee. The members of the committee discussed the scope of the fire
protection problem as they understood it. The discussion
was somewhat pointless and rambling until Klinger
seized the floor to propose the hiring of an expert con-
sultant to survey the situation for the committee. This
proposition was adopted at once. Later, on nomination
by Walter Strong, Klinger was elected chairman of the
committee. (Strong and Klinger, incidentally, were
classmates at Beloit College and graduated in the same
year.) Klinger in turn appointed a three man subcommittee to make recommendations for the hiring of
an expert to survey the school system. Jones urged the
group to move as rapidly as possible. He asked the
committee to make its final report by June 1, if possible,
so that the school board might consider it before draw-
ing up the school budget for the next fiscal year.

Despite the fact that he had appointed a subcommittee to find an expert, Klinger took over the job himself.
With some work he was able to compose a list of candidates for the job, the most promising of whom was
Robert I. Knudson, special representative of the Under-
writers' Service Association of Chicago. Knudson knew
the subject well, being a building inspector for his insurance industry employers, and he was even familiar
with Beloit's school buildings, since he had inspected
them in the past. Moreover, he was already under orders
to inspect the Beloit school system in the summer of
1959 and could be prevailed upon to advance his inspection tour by several months. This was opportune
because the inspection could be had at no cost to the
emergency committee. Klinger on his own initiative

invited Knudson to Beloit for an interview, and on the basis of the interview Klinger ceased to examine the qualifications of other candidates. Instead, Klinger invited the Chicago man to return to Beloit on April 18 to be present at the second full meeting of the emergency committee.

In the month between the March and April meetings Klinger also undertook a preliminary inspection tour of the schools on his own. Visiting every building, Klinger took note of the location of fire hydrants and their general character and the location of fire alarm boxes. From the findings of his tour he prepared a report to the emergency committee recommending the installation of a new hydrant at one school, the conversion of several hydrant outlets from smaller to larger sizes, and the installation or relocation of numerous fire boxes. He also proposed that poles on which boxes were located be painted with a wide red band for easy identification.

At the April meeting of the emergency committee, Knudson appeared and outlined his plans for inspecting the schools. He told the group that he would concern himself with matters of scholastic population, the numbers of children on each floor of the buildings, the width and placement of exits, the widths of corridors, obstructions to movement of personnel through corridors, and other matters of like nature. Apparently he had made contact with the Beloit fire department, for he announced that if he were chosen to make the inspections, Chief Fire Inspector Scodwell would accompany him on the tour. He promised to make the inspection in the latter part of April, and, on the basis of his proposals, was engaged. The committee received and adopted Klinger's report of hydrants and alarm boxes and directed that a copy be sent to the City Council with a request for action. Before adjourning, the committee inspected Hackett school and viewed a movie on fire

protection. The committee secretary duly prepared a
copy of the Klinger report and transmitted it to the
council.

The Klinger report got a chilly reception at the Municipal Center. City Manager Telfer at once referred
the document to Fire Chief Davis for review and comment. In a letter dated April 24, the fire chief noted
that a conference had already been held on the question of fire hydrants in school areas, and that the sense
of the conferees was that the existing hydrants were
adequate. As for the alarm box suggestions, the chief
was skeptical of their value. He noted that every school
building was equipped with telephones, and that telephone alarms were more satisfactory than box alarms.
He stated the department's position that, when it came
to saving lives, the alarm-hydrant situation was of sec-
ondary importance. Of primary importance were the
plans and procedures for school building evacuation.
On May 18 Manager Telfer put these comments, together with the Klinger report and the fire department
letter of January 26, in the hands of the council. The
council received the materials politely and made them
a part of the record. However, in the succeeding months
boxes were installed in, or moved to, the immediate
vicinity of every school building, without any public
fanfare.

As he had promised, Knudson made his tour of inspection accompanied by Scodwell at the end of April
and in early May. While waiting for the inspection and
report, the emergency committee made its own layman's
survey of the schools. Not all the members of the committee were present on each occasion; but all the schools
were viewed, and the committee members got some
first-hand information on their problem.

During the waiting period, School Superintendent
Jones wrote Chief Davis requesting fire department

recommendations on improvements which should be made at the several schools. Somewhat surprised by this request, Davis nevertheless answered on June 18. His letter was prepared with the assistance of Scodwell and in the light of Knudson's findings, of which Scodwell was aware.

The June 18 letter contained a program of fire protection broader in scope than had been suggested on January 26. First, Chief Davis urged immediate installation of sprinkler systems for the seven old elementary schools *and* in all the remaining buildings as money became available. Second, he recommended the enclosure of all open stairways with fire doors giving at least one-hour protection. Third, he asked for the installation of fire escapes wherever necessary. He did not repeat the recommendation regarding window screens, noting that this recommendation had already been complied with, nor did he say anything further about a monitoring system. In a telephone conversation soon afterward, Davis told Jones that the installation of an additional fire escape at Hackett School had been uppermost in his mind when he wrote out his third recommendation.

The following day Knudson sent his report to the emergency committee. The report was a bulky document and reflected painstaking effort. In a covering letter, Knudson made a general recommendation that sprinkler systems be installed in all schools and noted that the installation of fire alarm boxes at each school was under way.

The document for the most part was made up of building-by-building reports. Each followed a standard pattern: the name and location of the building was given; the character of the building was described; special fire hazards were delineated; and recommendations were set forth. In many, though not all, of the reports, Knudson proposed that stairways be enclosed

with approved materials and approved automatic-closing
fire doors on door openings. In specific instances he
proposed the adding of panic bars on doors leading
from buildings, the provision of additional fire extinguishers, the providing of exit lights, the removal of
hallway obstructions, the rehanging of doors to free
hallways of obstruction, and the providing of additional
outside exits.

As the June 1 deadline for reporting had passed,
School Superintendent Jones moved quickly to get the
Knudson report before the emergency committee. He
directed that members of his staff summarize the recommendations contained in the report and make cost estimates for each recommendation. On June 24 an un-
signed memorandum convening the emergency committee for a session on July 1 went out of Jones' office.
To reduce delays to a minimum Jones also circularized
the members of the school board to keep them informed
of developments.

The July 1 meeting of the emergency committee was
a long, tedious affair. Despite Jones' summarizing, the
Knudson report was too much to be digested at one
sitting. Moreover, the sum of the cost estimates was on
the order of a staggering $300,000. The emergency com-
mittee struggled with its task but had to be called back
into session on Monday evening, July 6, to get its work
done.

At this point the emergency committee had to face
up to the same problem which Davis and Scodwell had
wrestled with in January, namely, the financial condition
of the city. However desirable the adoption of the entire
Knudson program might be, few members of the
emergency committee felt that a $300,000 plan would
be received cordially. The committee, consequently,
adopted the same course Davis and Scodwell had

adopted and tempered its recommendations to seemingly hard necessities.

The committee's "tempering" proceeded by dividing the Knudson report recommendations into two groups: those which seemed immediately necessary and those which seemed less immediately necessary. The committee attached prime importance to (1) the installation of sprinkler systems in the seven old elementary schools, (2) the enclosure of the stairwells at the two junior high schools, and (3) the addition of panic bars, fire extinguishers, exit lights, fire doors, automatic-closing doors and metal lath-and-plaster ceilings where recommended in the report. It attached less importance to the installation of sprinklers in the two newest elementary schools, the enclosing of stairwells in all other multi-storied elementary schools, and the furnishing of additional fire escapes at the two junior high schools. On the basis of these judgments the emergency committee drafted a report of its own to the school board, urging the adoption of all the Knudson report recommendations but especially those items it considered of prime importance.

The school board met the following evening, July 7. Klinger was on hand to present the emergency committee reports. In light of the scope and importance of the report, the board agreed to meet in special session the following day at the Hilton Hotel, to which Klinger, Fire Chief Davis, and Chief Inspector Scodwell were invited.

The Hilton Hotel luncheon meeting turned out to be somewhat desultory and inconclusive. The entire Knudson report was canvassed, and the estimates for its complete adoption revised downward to approximately $280,000, but the feeling that the downward revision still left the cost of the entire program far too high led

the board members to review the priorities established
by the emergency committee. Board members were especially interested in the fire department's reaction to
the emergency committee's priorities. Pointed questions
put to Davis and Scodwell made both men uncomfort-
able, and very little information was elicited from them.
After the meeting, Board President Thompson prepared
a memorandum covering the essentials of the session
and circulated it among the members of the board and
the three councilmen who were also members of the
Joint Council-School Board Committee. (This joint committee, composed of three men each from both the
council and the school board, is a permanent committee
that exists for the purpose of keeping each organization
informed of the work of the other.)

The City Council, although it had not been officially
informed of the Knudson report nor of the emergency
committee recommendations based on it, knew that ultimately it would be asked for money to pay for some
new program. On July 20 it decided to call in Davis
and Scodwell for consultation. The two men, neither of
whom felt at ease, had the opportunity to review the
whole situation, starting with the Chicago fire tragedy.
They also had the opportunity to present their views on
what should be done in Beloit. In the discussion it was
brought out that up until the recent past the fire department had worked closely with school authorities in su-
pervising regular school fire drills, but such coöperation
did not at present obtain. The lack of coöperation was
deplored rather strenuously by council members, somewhat mildly and fatalistically by Davis and Scodwell.
Councilman Hanson asked obliquely about the emergency committee and its work. The tone of Hanson's
voice suggested that he was a bit resentful toward the
committee. Other members of the council, who had
been riffling through papers or listening perfunctorily,

noted this question with interest, but Davis' response to the question was, on the whole, noncommittal. He acknowledged the existence of the committee but said little about it. Council President Keenan moved that the matter be referred to the Joint Council-School Board Committee for additional study and that a representative of a firm manufacturing sprinkler systems be contacted to present estimates of the cost of sprinkler systems and their installation. The motion was duly seconded and passed.

Two weeks later the Joint Council-School Board Committee met for luncheon at the Hilton Hotel. Besides the committee members, City Manager Telfer and a representative of a Chicago sprinkler equipment firm, The Fyr-Fyter Company, attended. The Fyr-Fyter Company agent discussed sprinkler systems, the protection they furnish, and the approximate costs. As a result of the ensuing discussion the councilmen present became convinced of the value of sprinklers. Agreement was reached that Councilman Robert Tilley and the Fyr-Fyter agent would tour the city in the afternoon and take a preliminary look at some of the school buildings, as a step toward the drafting of specifications and calling for bids later. The results of this meeting were reported to the council on August 14 by Tilley, and the council viewed a movie demonstrating sprinkler equipment.

A second joint committee luncheon meeting was held at the hotel on August 19. Again Telfer appeared and, in addition, Fire Chief Davis. Board of Education President Thompson, who chaired the meeting, was determined to get some kind of agreement which he could carry back to the school board and which might have a reasonable chance of being accepted by the City Council. In opening the meeting Thompson noted that the school board was reluctant to consider any program less than the $280,000 program; however, the entire plan contemplated protection for buildings as well as protection for lives, and Thompson's major concern was the protection of lives. The discussion was rather delicate for, though virtually every person present felt that $280,000 figure needed paring down, none wanted the awesome responsibility which would be incurred in the suggesting of ways and means for its reduction.

In consequence, both school board and council members turned on the expert present, Davis. Davis was no happier at being on the spot than he had been a few weeks earlier. He steadfastly refused to lead the discussion about which items of protection were the most efficacious. Finally Thompson, in exasperation, started pairing items and asking point blank which of the two was the more important. To these questions Davis responded. Through a series of specific questions and specific responses Thompson was able to put together a list of five items, ranked in order of effectiveness and importance. Further discussion yielded little.

Just as the meeting was breaking up, Councilman Tilley spoke up and said that he had "something in the back of his head." He was not prepared to articulate the "something," but he asked the joint committee for a day or two to formulate his ideas. The other members were rather surprised but despite some misgivings agreed to the delay.

After sleeping on his idea, Tilley contacted Thompson. He proposed that the two highest items on the priority list which had been wrung from Chief Davis— installing a fire escape at Hackett School and sprinkler systems in the seven old elementary schools—be undertaken, and that the lesser items—purchase of additional extinguishers, new exit lights, addition of panic bars, etc.—be adopted for all the other schools. This latter suggestion was made partly, or even mostly, for public relations purposes. The suggestion caught Thompson's imagination, and he in turn worked up a concrete proposal. It was to all intents and purposes the same as the recommendations of the emergency committee, with the exception that for the enclosing of the stairwells at the junior high schools was substituted the erection of a fire escape at Hackett elementary school. The total cost of this program amounted to but $95,000. Thompson agreed with Tilley that it was a good idea for the plan to include something for every school, though his plan, in fact, failed to provide any items for one of the very new elementary schools and the senior high school.

This meeting of the minds was never referred back to the Joint Council-School Board Committee. Instead, Thompson got Jones to prepare a resolution embodying his and Tilley's ideas for immediate presentation to the school board. Thompson also referred to Jones the feeling of the council that building evacuation plans ought to be handled coöperatively by school authorities and fire department personnel. Presumably, this feeling had been conveyed to Thompson by Tilley.

On August 25 a special meeting of the Board of Education was held to act on the Thompson-Tilley accord. In all, the discussion and the voting on the proposition consumed little more than fifty minutes. The discussion was very mild, the members of the board merely trying to find out the exact nature of the accord. As the discussion reached a close, school board member Leo Hansen moved that the board ask the City Council to furnish $95,000 for the undertaking of the fire protection program, with the proviso that should less monies than the $95,000 be used on fire protection, the balance would go toward retiring the school's bonded indebtedness. Board President Thompson asked for a second. None was forthcoming. Hansen then moved that the Board of Education request the $95,000 for the program as outlined, and this motion was duly seconded. Before the final vote, an amendment was proposed to the effect that the school board adopt the entire school fire protection program "as suggested by the Fire Department." The amendment committed the board to the entire $280,000 program, which program was to be completed over a three-year period. Both the amendment and the original motion were adopted by unanimous vote.

The request for funds was transmitted by School Superintendent Jones to the council and was received on September 4. The city clerk prepared a resolution authorizing the school board to draw up plans and specifications and to advertise for bids to inaugurate the fire protection program. The authorization was moved by Councilman Hanson and carried by a unanimous roll call. No discussion occurred, and the council moved swiftly to the next order of business.

The plan thus inaugurated called for the installation of sprinkler systems in the seven old elementary schools, the erection of an additional fire escape at Hackett, and the equipping of most of the other buildings with some extinguishers, exit lights, panic bars, etc. The council took no notice of the amendment adopted by the school board to the effect that it wished to undertake the entire $280,000 program, nor of the implication that it would return hat-in-hand later for additional monies.

Thus, after nine months of deliberation, the city of Beloit decided how it would increase the protection of its schools and children against fire hazards. Clearly it was the catastrophic experience of another city which provoked Beloit to action, and it is apparent that the influence and advice of outside interests helped to determine what sort of action would be taken. Students of municipal government are occasionally inclined to discuss the subject of municipal policy making as though the city were isolated from any broader context. When this happens, the city is conceived to be a mere parallelogram of internal forces and policy, the result of the interaction of these forces only. This case suggests that this approach has decided limits.

The process by which the policy decision was made appears to have been democratic in the sense that there was adequate time and opportunity for participation by all interested parties. But democracy implies more than this. It implies that decisions are made by a responsible body whose actions are subject to popular review through proper procedures at appropriate times. It is open to question whether in this instance the council-manager structure fulfilled its theoretical promise to locate responsibility for decision clearly and firmly in the council. Certainly the council exercised its ultimate power of approval at the end of the process, and the council's feelings about spending during a business recession were taken into account all along the line. But even officially, in Beloit's particular situation, the council shares power and responsibility on school questions with the school board. On this rather technical question, the experts such as the firemen and insurance examiners should and did provide influential advice. And, since the general public interest was relatively keen and aroused, various leading and concerned private citizens were active participants in proposing policy. Surely it can be argued that, in the actual performance of the various groups and individuals involved, responsibility for the decision got mislaid somewhere in the general maneuvering.

7

The Case of the Bothersome Bees

Many Americans are politically unsophisticated. They know little of their governments or of governmental procedures and powers. They are not inclined toward speculation about what governments ought or ought not to do. They tend to be uncritical about Lincoln's famous dictum that "government should do for the people that which they can not do for themselves," as if this were a precise formula for determining when and under what circumstances government should act. On the other hand, they are prone to call on government for aid on the vague motive that "there ought to be a law," and this is especially true when they are engaged in disputes with their neighbors. In such circumstances these Americans do not speculate on the right and proper course for government to pursue, but they assume that because they want something, government's giving it to them is right and proper. This case illustrates such a situation.

The present case also illustrates a further major aspect

of policy making: namely, that the interests involved at the municipal level are by no means always, or even usually, organized group interests. The word "interests" in political science literature is used ambiguously to cover both (1) formally organized groups, the members of which share a common point of view and (2) a point of view which may be held by an individual or a number of diverse individuals not organized into a cohesive group. At the municipal level there are clashes of both kinds of interests, but a feature of local policy making is the high degree of interest conflict in which the interests are not organized groups but general points of view held by different people. In the present situation there was a pro-beekeeping interest and an anti-beekeeping interest; neither was organized in any sense. Clashes of interest are not less sharp for this lack.

Ernest Teeters is a retired carpenter who lives at the corner of Thunder Avenue and Dodd Place.* To occupy his days Teeters tends to his yard, which is one of the most beautifully kept yards in Beloit. He also tends to his garden, which is almost a show place, and keeps two hives of bees. Teeters' life is a quiet one and centered on these home-connected activities.

In the summer of 1959 Teeters' bees became a point of contention between him and several of his neighbors, especially between him and his next-door neighbor, Mrs. Thomas Walker. There is a history of hard feeling between Teeters and the Walkers, so this quarrel might be considered as only the latest in the line. To what extent Teeters' bees actually bothered Mrs. Walker and to what extent they served as a convenient pretext to renew the neighborhood feuding is a moot point.

* While the names of the public officials have not been changed, the names of the private citizens involved in this case have been altered, as have the names of the streets, etc.

Thinking that something ought to be done about the bees, Mrs. Walker contacted the city administration and complained about the bees' activities. The complaint was referred to Chief Sanitarian Stanley J. Goldschmidt, the head of the city's health department. (Wisconsin's laws on bees are rather interesting: the statutes do not protect people from bees, but, quite the contrary, they are written to protect bees from people.)

On receipt of the complaint Goldschmidt made a rather thorough investigation of the situation, visiting the scene of the dispute, inspecting the hives, talking with Teeters and Mrs. Walker, and searching the state statutes and city ordinances which relate to the subject. It seemed to Goldschmidt that the bees were fairly well behaved as bees go, and that their keeping was in order. As a result of his perusal of the law books, he found that there was no statute nor ordinance prohibiting the keeping of bees within the city limits. All things told, Goldschmidt could not see how he could proceed to take action against Teeters. In conference with Mrs. Walker he told her emphatically that as no law was being violated, he could do nothing. Rather wistfully, Goldschmidt hoped that this would end the matter.

Mrs. Walker was not at all satisfied by Goldschmidt's findings and conclusions and continued to push her point. This pushing led eventually to a broad conference between Mrs. Walker, City Manager Archie Telfer, City Attorney Gerald Noll, and Goldschmidt. Goldschmidt reviewed the entire case for the group. The question of the legality of keeping bees within the city limits was posed and directed to Noll. Without hesitation Noll concurred with Goldschmidt that no ordinance or statute was being violated. Rather wistfully, Telfer, Noll, and Goldschmidt hoped that this would end the matter.

Mrs. Walker, still unsatisfied, decided to appeal the

point to the City Council. Together with her husband she composed a letter to the council in which she related her grievances. She phrased the letter in the plural, hoping to circulate it through the neighborhood and round up additional support. The letter, dated October 5, was circulated, and four additional residents of the area signed it, along with their wives. The letter was forwarded to the city manager and through him to the council. Copies of the letter were directed to Council President Kevin Keenan and to City Attorney Noll. On Thursday night, December 3, the letter was laid before the council, then meeting as the Board of Public Works.

Mrs. Walker contended that the bees had been bothersome during the preceding summer, that they had accosted the children of the area while they were playing, that they had driven the residents of the area from their own gardens and prevented work therein, and that they had occasionally necessitated locking up the children's dogs. Mrs. Walker did not ask for any particular action but simply expressed the thought that any action taken by the proper officials would be appreciated.

When the Board of Public Works took up the subject, most of the members were unaware that there was a history to the case. The question of the law on the subject was immediately raised. Attorney Noll notified the board of the legal situation. Councilman Falco asked whether this could be prosecuted as a public nuisance. Noll replied that he didn't see how, as the matter affected too few people. He indicated that possibly the protest might be the basis of a civil suit. But inasmuch as this was beyond the interest of the board, the point was not pursued. Board Chairman Keenan then asked Noll to get together with "these people" and inform them of their rights. This seemed to dispose of the problem, and the board passed on to other matters. At no time did the board or its members seriously consider the possibility of taking formal action by enacting a bee-keeping ordinance.

So the problem rests in the lap of Attorney Noll. Goldschmidt too is still pondering the equities of the matter. He says he has found as a result of his years of public service that a public official has to be a peacemaker. As a consequence of this latest chapter in the bee dispute, he is currently poring over the terrain, searching for the road to peace. Of one thing are Noll and Goldschmidt certain: they have not heard the last of this topic. Nor, quite possibly, has the City Council.

This episode suggests several important questions. At what point does a problem among citizens assume enough importance to command the interest of a municipal government and formal action by a municipal council? Is the number of citizens involved the sole criterion? If not, then how much annoyance or damage must be suffered before governmental officials concern themselves, or councils act? Should some combination of the extent of the damage and the numbers affected determine governmental involvement, or some third, or even fourth, element determine it? If damages are considered to be the criterion, or a significant element of it, what kind of damages should be considered? Simply annoyance? Inconvenience? Or only monetary loss?

8

The Root of All Good

Underlying virtually all other problems confronting urban governments in America is the problem of money, its nurture and care. City councils everywhere must face the annual budget-making ordeal wherein they must determine the governmental services to be performed and the standards of service to be maintained, and whereby they hope they will find the money to pay for these services. Their spirits are very rarely buoyed up by the knowledge that most of the factors affecting their work of budget making are well outside their control.

In the division of labor among national, state, and local governments, cities are responsible for providing basic community services, which have grown in number and cost and in the standards of performance expected. Principal among these are police protection of persons and property; fire protection; construction and maintenance of streets and bridges; provision of adequate water supply; sewage disposal; operation of parks, libraries, and swimming pools; maintenance of hospitals and other health services and, directly or indirectly, of public educational facilities. In the past decade the effective performance of these functions has been gravely hampered by sharp rises in prices, population, and technical standards.

To finance this array of essential services, municipal governments have generally relied on the property tax, the only substantial source of revenue allotted to them, or left to them, by the states. In very recent years, in some states, city coffers have been augmented by grants and tax rebates from state treasuries. Of course, some supplementary funds are derived from such diverse sources as license fees, parking meters, and court fines. Some large cities may get federal funds for specific projects, and in a few states cities are permitted to levy a sales tax. But for most municipalities the tax on property—real estate, industrial machinery, and business inventories—remains the only significant source of money subject to decision and control by city councilmen.

It is at this point that the view of the citizenry, or that element of the citizenry which is politically effective, as to the proper role of the government in the community becomes important. Professor Oliver Williams has pointed out that communities differ on this question of the proper role of government,[1] and his discussion of four types of views is nowhere more significant or relevant than in this matter of budget making. Any given city's view of the proper role of government in the community is clearly reflected in the annual program its council conceives, and this in turn is reflected in the budget: the raising and spending of money.

Beloiters conceive of their government in caretaker

[1] "A Typology for Comparative Local Government," *Midwest Journal of Political Science*, V (May, 1961), 150-165.

terms, to use the most appropriate of Williams' types.[2] Beloiters want and expect their municipal government to carry on efficiently the traditional city services (plus, maybe, a few new services or extras), keep the tax rate down, and leave as much "freedom" to the individual as possible. As Williams points out, this implies a "pluralistic conception of the public 'good.'" It is certainly a conservative outlook for which Beloiters rarely make apology. The caretaker conception essentially sets the framework within which discussion of the city's taxing and spending policies proceed.

Beloit's civic leaders have pretty generally fought out the perennial fiscal battle along these conservative lines. Among Wisconsin's ten cities of 20,000 to 40,000 population (1950 census), Beloit has a lower public debt outstanding than six of them and a lower per capita expenditure and debt than five. Among the state's eighteen cities of over 25,000 population, Beloit's actual full value tax rate in 1960 was second from the lowest, $19.75 per $1,000 valuation as against an average of $26.05 for all Wisconsin cities. The city's bonded debt is about five million dollars, far below its legal limit of over thirteen million dollars. The city's credit standing is rated by the two leading investment advisory services as "Aa" and "A-1 plus," respectively. Furthermore, the soundness of this financial position is not based on the presence of any unusually great amount of taxable property.

Such conservatism in Beloit's financing is explained by several factors; perhaps basic among them is the cautious, conventional temper of its business and political leadership. But at least two special considerations keep

[2] Williams' four types and a somewhat more extensive discussion of them in relation to the Beloit situation can be found in the Introduction, 8-9.

the city under considerable pressure against high taxes. One is the fact that, as a heavy industry, capital-goods-producing center, Beloit is especially vulnerable to economic recessions, and the city authorities do not want to be caught in a period of business depression with their commitments overextended. The other is that, being located on the state line between Wisconsin and Illinois, the community must compete to attract business and industry not only with other Wisconsin cities but also with nearby cities in Illinois, a state which has no individual nor corporate income tax.

The city's fiscal year corresponds to the calendar year. The budget for each year is officially adopted and the tax rate set in the preceding December. And so every autumn the administrative officials of the city government and the school system begin to pull together from their various departments estimates of expenditures and receipts for the year to come. This is a tedious and complex business involving evaluation of current functions and programs, planning for new projects or organizational changes, and anticipation of costs for fifteen months ahead. The various department heads submit their proposals to the city manager or to the superintendent of schools, who then holds a series of consultations and informal hearings to evaluate, pare down, and coördinate the requests.

On the school side, the process has its complications. Account must be taken of parts of two different academic years to arrive at figures for the calendar year. Estimates must be made of tuition payments, of state aids which may be forthcoming as income, and of a few other small revenue sources. Funds for servicing a sizeable debt for past school-building must be included, as well as provision for a summer recreational program. Only then is the superintendent of schools in position to submit a tentative budget to the Board of Education, which reviews, modifies, and approves it. The school budget is still not final; it must yet satisfy the City Council, since only that body can levy the taxes it requires.

On the city side, there are other complications. Calculations of expenditures must include payments of principal and interest on the debt incurred for the building of hospitals, storm sewers, fire stations, and bridges. Estimates must be made of the income from a variety of fees, fines, and licenses, and of the probable "kickback," or rebate, from the state of Wisconsin of a part of the personal and corporate income taxes paid to the state by residents of Beloit City. (Wisconsin is one of the most generous of the states in rebating taxes to local governments.) The gap between proposed expenditures and probable income from these sources is, of course, the amount which must be raised by the general property tax levy. Only after all these calculations is the city manager, like his counterpart in the schools, in position to submit to the City Council a tentative budget for the municipal departments.

By mid-November the council has before it the several tentative budgets and all the necessary supporting figures and is ready to begin deliberations on the final budget. In addition to the school budget, which it receives from the Board of Education, and the municipal services budget, which it receives from the city manager, the council has handed to it bills from outside agencies, a part of whose income the council is required by Wisconsin law to raise through taxes. These include the city's share of the Rock County budget, a substantial sum for the local vocational school, and a small state reforestation tax. (It might be noted that the Rock County budget contains a small item for the state of Wisconsin. Thus, Beloit City, which receives considerable sums from the state by way of income tax rebate, must nevertheless tax its citizens' property and remit some of those revenues to the state!)

The council first sits with the city manager and informally reviews the city's own budget, cutting this item and perhaps adding to that, always holding in mind the other budgets which have been submitted to it. Very likely, when agreement is reached, the final amount to be raised by the property tax levy will be such as to bring the total tax rate to an even dollar or half-dollar figure and one not too far different from the rate levied the preceding year. Then a public hearing on the budget is announced for the first regular council meeting in December. Normally the hearing features statements of commendation or mild criticism by spokesmen of various groups in the city and by two or three individual citizens, and, unless the hearing produces startling new developments, the council formally adopts the budget and officially sets the total tax rate.

The budget-making process, while by all odds the most significant annual process, neither ends the matter of fiscal management nor exhausts the council's financial powers. During the year the council receives quarterly reports from the city manager on the financial standing of the city. As unanticipated problems and needs arise, the council will make minor adjustments by way of reallocating funds; but it will not reopen the tax rate question and cannot reduce amounts allocated to the schools, Rock County, the vocational school, and the state reforestation fund.

The budget-making process of 1959 for the fiscal year 1960 had its roots in the traumatic budgetary experience of the year before. The city's budgetary situation in 1958 was probably its worst in decades. In 1957-1958 the national economy went through a fairly serious recession, and Beloit was hit early and hard. As of the autumn of 1958 only the extremely optimistic were certain that the worst was over, and these optimists found no voice on the City Council. As always in such circumstances, the city was caught in a squeeze between falling income and rising expenditures, and the council was faced with the unhappy and unpopular alternatives of paring down governmental services, or substantially raising the property tax rate on already hard pressed homeowners and businesses, or perhaps doing both.

The first shock had come in the summer of 1958 when the tax assessor reported a decline in the property tax base, the "assessed valuation," from the 1957 figure of $66.9 million to $66.3 million. It was instantly perceived that to produce the same total tax monies as the year before, the *rate* of taxation on property would have to be raised. Furthermore, it would be necessary to reduce considerably the estimate of how much money the city would receive from the state as its portion of the 1958 Wisconsin individual and corporation income taxes collected from Beloit residents. The city administration's first guess was that this might be down from the $655,000 figure of 1957 to $378,000. Various other income figures would also be adversely affected by the recession situation. City councilmen were sharply aware that one dollar would have to be added to the current property tax rate of $45.50 per $1,000 valuation for every $66,000 lost from other sources, or added by way of new expenditures.

On the spending side, the council felt that it would be lucky to hold the city's own expenses at about the same figure as for 1958. The school population was expanding regardless of the recession, and the school district faced a cut of over $100,000 in state aids. But the biggest blow was expected from the county, since counties in Wisconsin carry a large share of the costs of welfare relief, a budget item which increases precipi-

tously during recessions. Rock County's refund from
state income tax would of course be down, and nearly
$300,000 had already been borrowed by that govern-
mental agency from its own general fund to cover un-
expected relief costs.

Financially, and politically, the situation appeared
critical. The Beloit Taxpayers' League was publicly and
deploringly anticipating a tax rise of $11 per $1,000
or even more, and as late as November 15 the *Beloit
Daily News* was viewing more calmly the prospect of a
$12 increase. The Taxpayers' League is one of the most
significant organized groups in the city as far as financial
affairs are concerned. It is a voluntary organization
of perhaps a hundred persons. Its chief concern is the
city's tax rate, but it also watches state and federal
spending and taxing closely. Although it is viewed by
the public as "ag'in everything," its spokesmen maintain
that it opposes only "unnecessary" taxes and tax increases. While its membership encompasses a broad
variety of persons and occupations, its most active members and guiding spirits are industrial executives, some
of them very highly placed in their respective company
hierarchies.

As the budgetary process actually developed in
1958, the economic and political outcome was serious
enough but not so desperate as some had imagined. The
demands on the city for contribution to the state reforestation fund and for maintenance of the vocational
school were only slightly higher than the year before.
The Rock County Board of Supervisors, in the face of
its own budget squeeze, decided to hold county spending to such a level that Beloit's share of the cost would
raise the city's total tax rate by only $2.71 per $1,000
valuation, from $10.19 to $12.90. In his tentative budget
the city manager proposed a modest $45,000 increase
in spending, and the council was able to trim the man-

ager's proposals to the point that the municipal services' budget actually showed a decrease of $60,000. On the revenue side, the council raised the manager's "guess" on the state's income tax rebate by a considerable $120,-000. In spite of these changes it still seemed necessary to boost the city's own share of the tax rate by $3.82 per thousand. The board of education also found its problems acute: with state aids down by $125,000, the board estimated its expenses up from $2.7 to $2.9 millions. This situation necessitated the board's requesting a tax rate of $32.37 a thousand, equivalent to a tax increase of $2.89. These were the figures in the budgets advertised for the council's public hearing of December 1, 1958, and together they spelled out a tax increase of $9.50 over the previous year's rate.

The council chamber was packed to overflowing for the public hearing. City Manager Telfer, in presenting the budget, called attention to the "dismal picture" on the revenue side, and warned that cuts in expenditures might make it impossible to provide all city services at their accustomed levels. For over an hour the council listened to spokesmen for industry, home owners, and the Taxpayers' League urge that spending be cut still further, while parents and teachers urged that no further cuts be made in the school budget. There was some sentiment among these parents and teachers for raising taxes even higher than was contemplated, if this would serve to maintain and advance the school system. Instead of acting immediately to set a tax rate, the council adjourned its meeting until the next Monday evening.

President Kevin Keenan of the council promptly contacted Board of Education President Dale Thompson and asked that the board review its budget and reduce its spending by approximately $66,000 so as to allow a cut of one dollar from the tax rate tentatively proposed. The council met informally and, while not cutting city spending further, agreed to apply about

$99,000 which remained in special parking meter and equipment replacement funds against the budget, thus permitting the proposed rate to be trimmed by $1.50. The Board of Education met on Friday evening. Reviewing its recommendations once more, it found it could cut its budget requests by only $9,000, and so notified the council.

On Monday evening, December 8, the council met early and informally to consider its course of action. After considerable discussion, a majority of the council agreed to set a tax rate of $52.50, which they could achieve by the cutting of the school budget by $66,000 as Keenan had requested of Thompson. At the appointed hour for the convening of the formal session, the councilmen took their seats in the official chamber and, without further discussion, except for an opportunity for each man to explain his vote, resolved adoption of the various budgets, and established the tax rate of $52.50. Five councilmen voted for the resolution; two councilmen voted against: Victor Emilson because he thought the cuts were too great and Gordon Merchant because the cuts were not great enough. President Thompson of the school board made a formal statement that the reduction in the school budget would work serious hardship on the school system. President Keenan answered for the council that the council had done its best.

The council's "best" was hardly pleasing to anybody. The seven-dollar tax increase, though less than the Taxpayers' League had expected, was still substantial. And it had been achieved by the elimination of virtually all capital improvements which many members of the city administration had hoped for. The school budget, while still providing for an across-the-board salary increase, called for a reduction in the annual dependency allowance from $400 to $300 for those teachers with dependents. Least happy of all was the Board of Education which was faced with the necessity of cutting $66,000 somewhere from its program, a task which it eventually accomplished with great travail. The Board of Education's first thought was to trim the school budget through a cutback on the athletic programs of the junior high schools and a cutback, or the elimination, of the kindergarten programs at the elementary level. Public reaction—and a cry of "politics" from offended City Council members—made this unfeasible. Ultimately, at the suggestion of school administrators, the cuts were made in such items as furniture replacement and building maintenance.

The 1958 budgetary crisis had some political repercussions, most overtly in the council elections of April 1959. In January 1959 Councilmen Keenan and Schultz, two of the five-man majority on the budget vote, decided to stand for reëlection. The third, Councilman Emilson, whose term was expiring, had decided to retire from office and publicly announced his intention. Five other candidates, some of them put forward or supported by various "progressive" and pro-school individuals and groups, filed nomination papers for places on the election ballot. For a few weeks the campaign, which had developed into a warm contest, looked as though it would be a referendum on the budget, and more particularly on the cut in the Board of Education's proposed budget requests. In the middle of the campaign, however, the situation was confused by the development of other "issues" and by the maneuverings of several rare alliances, including that of one major industry with Beloit's leading labor union. On election day a full half of the registered voters turned out, an unusually large turnout for municipal elections in Beloit. The outcome left considerable room for interpretation: Keenan and Schultz led the field of seven and were reëlected; the third seat was captured by Beloit College professor Harry R. Davis, who had originally been backed by many of the dissident forces but was endorsed by some downtown business elements in latter stages of the canvass.

The 1958 budgetary crisis and the elections also left some scars and bitterness, especially on certain council-school board relationships, which were not assuaged for a period of five months. During the spring of 1959 the board asked the council for a special appropriation of $45,000 for the hiring of an architect to prepare plans and specifications for a new and badly needed junior high school. The request gave rise to some "misunderstandings." Late in May the two groups held a joint meeting of an hour and a half in length, following one of the council's regular meetings. Though some effort was made to confine the discussion to the request at hand, the conversation ran the whole gamut of school matters. The Board of Education wanted quick action on its request, but it was doomed to frustration. The council was not prepared to act.

During the middle months of 1959 city councilmen watched for evidences of economic recovery which would signal a relaxation of pressure on local finances. Foremost in their minds was the size and timing of a major bond issue to finance the new junior high school, a new fire station, an emergency treatment room for the hospital, and—as it turned out—increased fire protection for some school buildings. Convincing signs of recovery, both nationally and locally, could produce the votes necessary to authorize proceeding with plans for these projects and would give guidance to city and school administrators in planning their budgets for

1960. The council asked City Manager Telfer for a preliminary budget survey by June 15. In the absence of any very reliable figures, Telfer persuaded the council to delay its budget review until early autumn.

The summer did produce some encouraging developments. Nationally, the economy was turning upward, and, at home, the Beloit tax assessor announced an increase in the city's assessed property valuation of over three-quarters of a million dollars. Better yet, when the state of Wisconsin returned Beloit's share of the income tax collected earlier in the year, the return was over $150,000 higher than the council had estimated. This return not only relieved the current budget, permitting such actions as the payment of a snow-removal deficit and the restoring of special funds which had been "raided," but also encouraged a higher estimate of income tax rebate for the following year. It was at this point that the council authorized the school board to proceed with its plans for increasing fire protection in the schools to the amount of $95,000, this action suggesting a softening of feelings on the part of the council toward the Board of Education.

During September the budgetary wheels began to turn slowly. Department heads were starting their annual review of programs and planning increased spending requests for 1960. One evidence of this latter point was the City Council's receipt of memoranda from special committees of the police and fire departments, respectively, making a case for a $50-a-month pay raise across the board for police and fire department personnel—followed by a calming memo from City Manager Telfer. The council also received its requested preliminary budget survey from the city finance officer, who was also the city clerk; this was a very conservative document which estimated decreases in revenue and

increases in spending at the county, school and municipal levels and indicated a total tax rate increase of five
dollars per thousand.

Meanwhile, school administrators and the Board of
Education were engaged in the same sort of activity. Not
only did the increasing scholastic population and its
attendant problems dictate an increased budgetary request, but the improvement in the economic situation,
as indexed by the increase in the total assessed valuation of city property, seemed to justify it. More particularly, earlier in the year the legislature of Wisconsin
had generously increased the formula for state aid to
school districts, and the Beloit district stood to profit
by the change. As the estimates were compiled, the
superintendent of schools and the Board of Education
began to envision an increased spending on the order
of $250,000, which increase would include an across-
the-board salary increase of $250 for the teachers.

However, a certain aura of caution pervaded the
work of department heads and school officials, especially
the latter. What appeared to be an upturn of the economy in September might prove to be a false dawn by
December. Neither then nor in recent years has there
been sufficient commitment to long-range planning of
public programs, either municipal or scholastic, to give
rise to a "catching-up" outlook. Projects eliminated in
1959 would not automatically be "made up" in 1960
by an increased rate of spending in the latter year. The
members of the Board of Education were pretty generally satisfied with asking for an increase of $250,000,
especially in light of the fact that with the increased
state aid the amount to be raised locally by the property
tax was relatively insignificant. Indeed, once the school
tax rate of the preceding year were applied to the increased property valuation, it would raise almost the
exact amount needed.

At its regular meeting on October 5, the council took action indicative of some confidence in the future. It authorized the board of education to proceed with preparation of plans and specifications for the new junior high school. At the same time it directed the city manager to do the same for the new fire station and for the emergency facilities at the hospital. But the intention was clear that the bond issue covering these projects would not be issued until 1960, thus keeping any principal payments off the budgets for that year.

In late October and early November the board of supervisors of Rock County carried out its deliberations on the 1960 budget. The county was found to be in a much improved situation; it, too, had received a higher income tax rebate from the state than anticipated, and the county welfare department was spending much less for relief than had been authorized. After some maneuvering about salary increases for county personnel and about how much of its general fund surplus to apply against the new budget, the county board reached its decision. A total county tax levy of $2.4 million was adopted, a decrease of nearly half a million dollars from the previous year. Herman Schultz, a member of the county board as well as of the Beloit City Council, immediately announced that this action would reduce the Beloit tax rate by at least $2.25.

President Keenan called an informal budget session of the City Council for the evening of November 23 in the conference room of the Municipal Center. All seven councilmen attended, as well as City Manager Telfer and City Finance Officer and Clerk Calland. All budgets except the city's own for municipal services were already authorized, and the tax rate would be unchanged by requests from the Board of Education, the vocational school, and the state reforestation fund. The final figure from Rock County amounted to a reduction in the rate of $2.58. Telfer had previously mailed the councilmen his own tentative municipal services budget.

At Keenan's suggestion, the city manager pointed out the salient features of his proposed municipal services budget. He noted that he was applying $50,000 of the current year's unexpected income tax apportionment on the income side. As for 1960, he estimated the income tax rebate at $752,000 (about $100,000 more than actual receipts for 1959) and the revenue from the general property tax, assuming no change in the rate for municipal services, at $385,000 (about $20,000 higher than in 1959). With the extra funds available Telfer proposed raising the salaries of police department, fire department, and other personnel by over $50,000 (thus awarding fire and police department personnel a $25 a month increase), installing a long-awaited passenger elevator in the Municipal Center, and making a number of smaller capital purchases and adjustments in municipal spending. Total expenditures would increase by $140,000.

While no provision was made for it in the budget, Telfer and Calland strongly recommended the creation of a $100,000 "tax stabilization fund." Calland, to whom the project particularly appealed, argued that surpluses in good years could and should be placed in such a fund to become available for use in bad years. Such a kitty would render unnecessary an inordinate rise in the property tax rate, such as had occurred the year before, and would render less disastrous a miscalculation of any one of the sources of income, as for example, the state's income tax rebate. While the several members of the council listened politely, none of them made a motion in support of Calland's proposition.

After brief discussion the councilmen were generally agreed that Telfer's budget should not be radically changed, and that the tax rate should be cut to $50, still permitting the city to spend eight cents of the "saving" made possible through the cut in the county rate. No formal discussion occurred on the possibility of keeping the higher rate of the previous year and further expanding services or paying debts. The assumption generally acquiesced in was that if some modest improvements on the city's side could be made (the council would never consider suggesting increased school expenditures, as this was the business of the Board of Education) and some cutback from the large tax rate increase of 1958 could still be made, then that should be done. Feeling rather comfortable fiscally, the councilmen began a line-by-line review of the budget, raising questions and making suggestions at will. Only minor changes were agreed to by a majority of the council; no formal votes were taken and no official record was kept. The council's changes, along with other minor adjustments later made administratively, raised the total of spending by $24,000. This increase was to be paid for in part by the eight cents "saved" on the county rate; the council instructed Calland to raise the rest by adjusting upward the state tax apportionment estimate!

On November 25 City Manager Telfer released the revised budget and tax figures to the press and public. At the same time he gave the press a statement at once triumphant and apologetic in tone. After explaining the budget in general terms the manager commented briefly on particular items. With regard to the budgeted $52,000 for increased salaries for city employees, Telfer stated: "We consider this increase barely sufficient to compensate for the increased cost of living since January 1, 1958, when present wage and salary rates were set." Concerning an item for the replacement of a twenty-seven-year-old pumper for the fire department, he noted that the pumper was considered inadequate for further use. He noted, further, that the budget contained no items for the municipal hospital or golf course, which were largely self-sustaining, and added: "Efforts are being made to make the ambulance service self-supporting so this can also be eliminated from a property tax subsidy in another year." "Good news," cheered Walter Strong, editor of the local newspaper, with regard to the prospective cut in taxes.

The public hearing on the budget was held on December 7, on the occasion of a regular council meeting. The council chamber was fairly well filled with citizens at the time of the hearing, though the crowd shrank a bit in size when President Keenan announced that a controversial rezoning request had been withdrawn. Moving the budget hearing up to first place on the agenda, Keenan announced that the council had the intention of adopting the budgets and establishing the tax rate as published. He then invited comments from the audience. The only person to accept the invitation was a representative of the Taxpayers' League, who praised the council for a welcome cut in taxes. The council then proceeded to adopt, by unanimous roll call vote, a resolution approving the budgets and levying the property tax rate at $50 per $1,000. The whole business was completed in five minutes and the council resumed its regular agenda. At the council meeting on December 22, ordinances were adopted raising the salary scales of city employees.

"All of us, however, must be appreciative," commented the editorial writer in the *Beloit Daily News* two days later, "of the work of City Manager A. D. Telfer, his aides and councilmen in 'holding the line' wherever possible to give residents a $50 tax rate. This is a reduction of $2.50 per $1,000 valuation over last year's rate, and the savings to taxpayers came just in time for Christmas."

The decisions which shaped Beloit's budget in 1959 cannot be understood apart from knowledge of the difficult budgetary experience of the previous year; and both together are required to provide a picture which approximates the "typical" or "representative" municipal budget-making process. The contrast between the two experiences, however, may be more apparent than real. For each may be properly understood and analyzed only in the light of the basic conservative, or caretaker, conception of government held by Beloiters. Objectively the budget situations of 1958 and 1959 seem quite different: in the former year outside revenues were shrinking rapidly and expenditures increasing; in the latter, revenues were rising and rising more than enough to take care of the moderate spending increases which were proposed. But the approach of the council to the two situations was essentially the same—a hold-the-line strategy dictated by the caretaker conception. In both years, for better or for worse, the council's decisions appear to have been delimited by this psychological-political factor, leaving unexplored the broader areas of discretion permitted by economic and legal limitations. In this microcosm the much-discussed issue of whether the nation is adequately supporting the "public" sector of its economy was not formally considered.

Substantively, this case suggests the broad and basic issue whether governmental functions and financial resources are properly distributed among local, state, and national levels. Do Beloit's fiscal instabilities illustrate the need for realignment of this historically "given" distribution?

Beloit's budgetary experience offers some further insights into the decision-making process. A host of officials, political and administrative, participated in the budget making. The student should attempt to assess the relative influence of administrators and politicians in the total activity. Related questions arise. What would appear to be the principal values, pressures, and interests operative in budget making? Who should participate in deliberations at various points in the process? When, if ever, should meetings be closed to the public? Finally, is not the governing of men a less rational and systematic, a more "human," process than is generally supposed?